Teen.

What's your guy-Q?

and other quizzes to help discover the real you!

Beth Mayall

SCHOLASTIC INC.
New York Toronto London Auckland Sydney
Mexico City New Delhi Hong Kong

ISBN 0-439-11466-7

Distributed under license from
The Petersen Publishing Company, L.L.C.
Copyright © 2000 The Petersen Publishing
Company, L.L.C. All rights reserved.
Published by Scholastic Inc.

Produced by 17th Street Productions,
an Alloy Online, Inc. company
33 West 17th Street
New York, NY 10011

Teen is a trademark of Petersen
Publishing Company, L.L.C.

SCHOLASTIC and associated logos are trademarks and/or
registered trademarks of Scholastic Inc.

12 11 10 9 8 7 6 5 4 3   3 4 5

Printed in the U.S.A.   01
First Scholastic Printing, July 2000

For Drew, who knows me better than I know myself. (Poor guy)

introduction

all about these quizzes

When the cutie you're crushing on launches a gummi bear into your drink at lunch, you would: (a) dump the juice in his lap, (b) scoop out the bear and eat it with a smile, or (c) roll your eyes at his oh-so-obvious flirtation. . .

So what's it gonna be? No pressure or anything, but the answer you pick will reveal a lot about you—and that's just one question!

With the thirty-three quizzes in this book, you'll get a glimpse of your deepest feelings about boys, your friends, your family, and yourself. Plus you'll discover some amazing qualities you never knew you had, as well as some sneaky ways to improve your fabulous self.

Now on to the quizzes!

1

all about
guys, love
& dating

sly. baffling. unexplainable.
Although it sounds like an episode of
The X-Files, we're really talking about
the insanely kooky signals guys send
out. You know how you're positive a
guy likes you one minute, but then you
think he hates you because of that
reeeally slimy spitball he shot at you?
(Ew.) And then there's the flip side—
how you're charming and oh-so-cool
around your friends but turn into a
complete nervous wreck when your
crush is even in the same zip code?
The quizzes in this chapter will help
you decode, decipher, and debaffle-ize
these behaviors, along with revealing
your unique love personality. So if
you're ready, let's take a walk through
the guy mind. (Leave your good shoes
at home.)

1. What's your guy type?

Do you swoon over the sweetie next door? Or is a quiet, soulful poet more your speed? These questions will help you discover what kind of guy will melt your heart.

1. If you had to put together the ingredients for a perfect date, you would add

    (a) loud music, dancing, and a really late curfew.
    (b) a movie, hand-holding, and serious cuddle time.
    (c) a hike, casual clothes, and beautiful surroundings.

2. Surprise! Proving that he is in fact the sweetest guy in the world, your guy shows up at your doorstep with flowers. What kind would they be?

    (a) A mehndi tattoo with your name written in flowers on his hunky bicep.
    (b) Long-stemmed roses.
    (c) Wildflowers that he picked himself.

3. It's dirt-dishing time on girls' night out. What do you think they would say about your dream sweetie the second you run off to the bathroom?

    (a) "Have you ever heard of any of those bands he's always talking about?"
    (b) "That guy is sooo whipped."
    (c) "I think he hates us—he never comes around."

4. When you and your guy have a romantic dinner, just the two of you, how does the conversation go?

(a) You mostly talk about other people—friends, teachers, or kids at school—and music, TV, or movies.

(b) You mainly chat about each other—how nice the other looks, how much you like each other.

(c) You take turns opening up about your deepest thoughts—what you dreamed last night, how you wish you were more like your older sister. . . .

5. It's his turn to pick the movie, your turn to choose the snack. What tickets does your dream guy buy while you eye the Milk Duds?

(a) Something action packed or scary.

(b) A romance, comedy, or drama.

(c) An independent movie that most people have never heard of.

SCORING

Now count up the number of times you selected each letter. Read the answer section below the letter you selected most often.

IF YOU CHOSE MOSTLY A'S: **You're Hunting for a Hot Hipster**

His uniform: It's gotta be trendy. He sports an awesome hairdo, and you think he might own more pairs of shoes than you do.

His habitat: Often spied at music stores or the mall.

What you'll love about him: He knows all the cool places to go, and he's invited to every party in town. As his date, you will be, too. Since he makes a grand entrance anywhere he goes, your popularity level just might go up.

What you'll hate about him: Eventually you'll crave a romantic night alone so you can get to know the inner him, but he's all about checking out the local scene.

How to snag this sweetie: If music's your thing, there's your perfect conversation topic. Or if you're kinda shy about chatting him up, you could just enter his orbit on the dance floor.

IF YOU CHOSE MOSTLY B'S: **You're Blown Over by the Boy Next Door**

His uniform: Straight outta Abercrombie & Fitch and the Gap.

His habitat: You'll see him at sporting events (in the audience or on the court or field) or hanging around your house.

What you'll love about him: This sweetie is the perfect gentleman—always ready for hand-holding or back rubbing. He's interested in your feelings, your friends, and your family.

What you'll hate about him: He isn't exactly a wild man, so if you're looking for spur-of-the-moment excitement, you might have to give him a week's notice . . . and a detailed itinerary.

How to snag this sweetie: Invite him to one of your sporting events or go check out one of his. If he's less jock and more sofa slug, invite him over for a Blockbuster night or Sega match.

IF YOU CHOSE MOSTLY C'S: **You're Scamming on the Private Poet**

His uniform: Casual and totally original. He pulls off a look that most guys couldn't.

His habitat: He loves the outdoors, and he grooves on spending time alone, so this specimen may be hard to locate.

What you'll love about him: He's so smart and sensitive. Being his soul mate would be deeply spiritual.

What you'll hate about him: He's kind of a loner, so chances are he wouldn't be into double dates with your friends.

How to snag this sweetie: Share something personal, like your artwork or creative writing. Ask him what he thinks.

2. What's your crushing style?

Sure, it's safe to scam on your sweetie from afar. But some girls are cool with doing the chasing. Do you like to be the cat or the mouse? Find out with this quiz.

1. You've had a serious crush on a guy who never knew your name.
True: *Go to 3*   **False:** *Go to 2*

2. Just about everybody knows who you like.
True: *Go to 4*   **False:** *Go to 5*

3. You would bet that your crush has no idea you like him.
True: *Go to 6*   **False:** *Go to 5*

4. If you like a guy, you would dig up his phone number—and use it!
True: *Go to 7*   **False:** *Go to 8*

5. Your major crush of the moment is a celebrity.
True: *Go to 6*   **False:** *Go to 8*

6. You're usually attracted to a guy's looks before you know his personality.
True: *Go to 9*   **False:** *Go to 8*

7. You always make an effort to get to know your crush's friends.
True: Go to 10   **False:** *Go to 11*

8. You change crushes almost as frequently as you change nail polish.
True: Go to 7   **False:** *Go to 11*

9. You sometimes lose interest when your crush starts liking you back.
True: Go to 12   **False:** *Go to 11*

10. You almost always do the asking when it comes to first dates.
True: Go to Go-Get-Him Girl   **False:** *Go to 13*

11. You're good friends with at least one guy you used to have a crush on.
True: Go to Cool-Crushin' Chica   **False:** *Go to Slow-Motion Sistah*

12. If you heard through the grapevine that your crush wanted to get to know you better, you would wait for him to make the first move.
True: Go to Slow-Motion Sistah   **False:** *Go to Cool-Crushin' Chica*

13. Your friends would say you usually become obsessed with your crushes.
True: Go to Go-Get-Him Girl   **False:** *Go to Cool-Crushin' Chica*

SCORING

Go-Get-Him Girl
Props to you for pursuing what you want—you're aggressive and proud of it, thankyouverymuch. But if you ever

start to feel like your boy-snagging moves are just a little too aggressive, you could easily take a step back and still get great results. At the moment it seems like much of your attention is focused on your potential love instead of on your friends or (even better!) yourself. Give the boys a chance to crush on you for a while. But if you're spicing on a sweetie who seems too shy to take the first step, don't be afraid to use your smooth moves. After all, a cool girl like you shouldn't sit home and wait for the phone to ring.

Cool-Crushin' Chica

You aren't afraid to let a guy know you're interested—but you'll only do that once you're sure that you like him. You actually take the time to get to know a guy before you decide you're gaga, and that will save you some major heartache. Plus, since you become friends with a guy without revealing your crush, you'll be sure there's chemistry before anybody makes a move. Can you share your secrets with the rest of us, pretty please?

Slow-Motion Sistah

You probably find that once you get to know some of your crushes, you aren't really crushing anymore. Could it be that your standards are so impossibly high that you lose interest once you see a guy isn't perfect? Hmmm—maybe. It's also possible that you haven't met the right guy yet—or maybe you just aren't lookin' for love at the moment. That's fine—

there's no rush. But just in case, you might want to take a second look at your boyfriend criteria and make sure you aren't eliminating primo sweeties for silly reasons.

3. Do you know how to flirt?

Is the vibe you're sending guys more friendly than flirty? Or could your charming ways be a little over the top? Find out with this quiz.

DIRECTIONS: Grade each statement with a **1** (if it's totally unlike you), **2** (if it's sort of like you), or **3** (if it's so like you, it's scary).

1. You have no problem asking a guy out.
2. When your crush has a glob of ketchup on his chin, you reach up and wipe it off.
3. You always laugh at jokes, even if they aren't that funny.
4. You feel comfy play wrestling your friend's boyfriend.
5. You'd be embarrassed if your parents knew how you interacted with guys.
6. You touch people frequently when you talk.
7. Everyone knows that you're a hugger.
8. You're good at remembering people's names.
9. You're known for being shocking or talking about off-limits topics.
10. In a coed game of truth or dare, you always pick dare.

11. When you have a boyfriend, you kinda like making him jealous.

12. At parties you spend way more time talking to guys than girls.

13. You turn on the charm around all guys—even ones you don't have feelings for.

14. You wear tight clothes that show off your body because it gets you attention from guys.

SCORING

Add up the numbers you wrote in the blanks above and read the answer section next to your total below.

IF YOU SCORED 14 TO 24: **Friendly Yet Flirty**

Your motto: I'm just one of the guys.

Your smoothest move: Slyly becoming your boy toy's close friend and waiting for him to realize that you're not just cool—you're cute, too.

Your recurring nightmare: Hel-lo? Can guys be any more clueless? It seems that your charms may be a little too subtle to catch certain cuties' attention. You might have to turn up the flirty vibes just a couple of notches. Like (gulp!) asking him to hang out after school or seeing if you can bribe a friend into putting in a good word for you. Don't worry—it isn't you. Some guys are just thickheaded that way.

IF YOU SCORED 25 TO 34: **Charming with Caution**

Your motto: I'll let him know I'm interested, but I won't throw myself at him.

Your smoothest move: Those slick, did-she-mean-to-do-that touches that leave a guy interested but wondering whether you reeeally like him.

Your recurring nightmare: Being nice is, well, nice. But have you ever noticed that some guys misinterpret your just-plain-friendliness for flirtation? Make sure that you aren't sending mixed signals to guys you aren't looking for love with. For example, keep the playful touches to a minimum and throw around the word *friend* a lot in your conversations. But when you do dig the boy? Work that magic.

IF YOU SCORED 35 TO 42: **Dangerously Devious**

Your motto: If he has a pulse, he's worth chatting up.

Your smoothest move: You make every guy in the room feel ultraspecial by showering them with attention.

Your recurring nightmare: Have you ever noticed that the guy you really have feelings for never makes a move? That's because he sees you flirting with all the other guys—he can't tell if you really like him or if he's just one of the crowd. If you want to make a specific boy feel special, you may need to tame your flirtatious streak when he's around. Also, notorious flirts like you often have problems with their girlfriends. You need to realize that certain guys are off-limits—and that list includes friends' crushes and boyfriends.

4. What's your guy-q?

When it comes to figuring out boys, are you so on target, it's eerie . . . or so off, it's scary? Check out these questions and see how well you know how to read the male mind!

1. On your first dinner date with a guy, you should order

(a) whatever you want, even if it's the most expensive thing on the menu.

(b) something light, like a salad, and not eat much of it.

(c) something you like, but steer clear of stinky stuff like garlic, just in case.

2. When the convo rolls around to the topic of your dating history, most guys want to know

(a) a few details—like how long you dated and whether you're still friends.

(b) nothing, because it's in the past and you're going out with a new guy now.

(c) almost everything—especially how you broke up.

3. You meet an amazing guy at the skate park. After an entire day of hanging out and flirting, you give him your number and tell him to call. Then you go home and sit by the phone and wait . . . and wait . . . and wait. After a week passes and he still hasn't called, you assume

(a) he has a girlfriend and was just messing with your mind.

(b) he must have lost your number, or he's trying to build up the nerve to call you.

(c) he wasn't really interested but didn't want to hurt your feelings.

4. When you pass a guy in the hall and he immediately makes a major show of clowning around with his friends (and barely makes eye contact with you), it probably means

(a) he's letting you know he isn't into you by blowing you off.

(b) he's interested in you but doesn't know what to do about it.

(c) he was just about to talk to you, but one of his friends distracted him.

5. You can tell that a guy has a major crush on you when

(a) he gets a little nervous talking to you, but he always has something to say.

(b) he talks about you for hours with his friends.

(c) he constantly teases you and calls you mean names.

6 You're Jewel's number-one fan, so when you win tickets to her concert, you're on cloud nine. During the show your date is practically falling asleep in his chair—but afterward he says he had fun and suggests getting coffee together. What does this mean?

(a) He's just so relaxed around you that he felt comfortable and snuggly.

(b) He's not so hot on Jewel and feels bad about falling

asleep, so he wants to make it up to you by going out for coffee.

(c) You've officially bored him into a coma, and he needs caffeine to jump-start his brain.

7. In the hall you spy your crush chatting with another girl. She's giggling really loudly and hanging all over him, and he seems to be eating it up. If you want to snag his attention during your next convo, your best bet is to

(a) act normal and talk about something you have in common.

(b) get a little more giggly and flirty since you know he likes that.

(c) make an inside joke about the giggly girl who was glued to him to show him you're secure.

First see how your answers measured up to what real guys revealed (hint—the two-point answers are the high guy-Q picks). Then add up your score and check out the paragraph under your total to get your personal guy-Q reading.

1. **a = 1, b = 3, c = 2**

Guys we polled said that it actually freaks them out when girls don't eat. "I feel like a dork sitting there pigging out if she isn't eating anything," says Josh, 17.

2. **a = 2, b = 3, c = 1**

No need for full disclosure, thanks—you aren't applying to the FBI. "I like to hear when a girl is friends with some of her exes," says Brian, 16. "It means she doesn't go psycho if things don't work out. But I definitely don't need a play-by-play of the whole relationship."

3. a = 3, b = 1, c = 2
Sorry, but unless he's ultra-shy, 99.999 percent of the time he didn't lose the number—he just wasn't interested in you that way. "It's not like you can say no when a girl just hands you her number. But if I liked her, I'd be glad that she did it," says Chris, 18.

4. a = 3, b = 2, c = 1
Most guys won't show they're into you when their friends are around. "If I went up to her and she blew me off right in front of all my friends, they'd laugh their heads off," says Josh. So if he ignores you, it may actually be a good sign.

5. a = 2, b = 1, c = 3
Girls sit around and gab about their crushes. Guys don't. "I'll make comments to my friends if I think a girl is hot," says Matthew, 19. "But if I really like someone, I'll try to talk to her alone."

6. a = 1, b = 2, c = 3
Consider it a compliment that he endured three hours of torture with you—it means he likes you. "Once I really liked this girl and she made me go to the opera with her. I went because I wanted to be with her, but she could totally tell that I hated it," says Brian.

7. a = 2, b = 3, c = 1
Don't stoop to being catty, and don't clone the girl, either. "It's fun to talk to girls who flirt a lot, but I'd never go out with somebody like that. She'd get annoying," says Matthew, age 16.

IF YOU SCORED 7 TO 10: **Your Guy-Q: Living in La-La Land**

Your world must be a dreamy place to live. You always find a way to put a positive spin on his signs—even the ones that clearly aren't good. It's definitely time for a lesson in guy-speak. One good way to pick up the language is to start making more guy friends—they'll clue you in fast. And when you stop making excuses for the guys you want to like you, you may notice some sweeties whose true I-like-you signals you were missing.

IF YOU SCORED 11 TO 16: **Your Guy-Q: Roaming in Reality**

You are so fluent in boy talk, you could write a dictionary for your less-clued-in friends. It's rare that you miss signals boys send your way, and you know that by acting like yourself, you help put their nerves at ease—because the truth is, they're just as clueless about the opposite sex as you are! Use these amazing decoding powers to help your friends read their crushes—or maybe even consider writing that dictionary. (It would be a best-seller!)

IF YOU SCORED 17 TO 21 **Your Guy-Q: Tiptoeing Over Thorns**

Ouch! Your answers are a major warning that the treatment you're getting from guys is pretty rotten. You expect them to send out nasty signals—and when they do, you convince yourself that's normal. Trust me on this one—not all guys are jerks. So if you think you have to put up with a guy who teases or ignores you, think again. Maybe your boy blindness comes from the fact that you just haven't met that many nice guys—and that's an easy thing to fix. Instead of hunting for a hottie to smooch, get friendly with a guy you dig on a just-friends level. It'll show you how sweet guys can be, and that'll boost your expectations.

5. Are you relationship ready?

Movie dates . . . wearing his big, cuddly sweatshirt . . . finding a bouquet of flowers in your locker . . . Sure, having a boyfriend is fun—but it takes a lot of work and commitment. Can you handle the game of love? Get ready to find out.

DIRECTIONS: Check off all the statements that sound like you.

1. When you have a fight with the guy you're dating, you talk about it to him instead of your best girlfriend.

2. All of your friends have boyfriends, and you feel left out.

3. The only boy you would even consider dating is on MTV.

4. You'd be cool staying in on a night when your boyfriend didn't feel like going out.

5. You're completely busy. Even your family barely sees you.

6. You recently broke up from a long relationship.

7. Having a boyfriend would guarantee that you have plans every weekend.

8. You're generally happy with yourself as you are.

9. When a guy asks what your middle name is, you wonder why he's getting so personal.

10. You've gone on a few dates, and you know what kind of guy you're looking for.

11. When you get upset, you don't yell and scream.

12. There's a guy in your life who you really like— and not just because he's popular or has a car. And he seems to like you, too.

13. You've thought about sex and how you would deal with it if a guy pressured you to do it before you were ready.

14. Guys are like crayons—a box of sixty-four is better than just one.

15. You would split your social time evenly between your girlfriends and your boyfriend.

16. You have a few clubs, hobbies, and activities that you're passionate about.

SCORING

Count up your points using the answer key below, then read your answer section.

GIVE YOURSELF TEN POINTS FOR EACH CHECKMARK NEXT TO THESE STATEMENTS: 1, 4, 8, 10, 11, 12, 13, 15, 16
SUBTRACT FIVE POINTS FOR EACH CHECKMARK NEXT TO THESE STATEMENTS: 2, 3, 5, 6, 7, 9, 14

IF YOU SCORED UNDER 30: **First-Rate Friend**

Sounds like you're ready for a lot of things—hanging out with your friends, working your butt off at school, scoping out cute guys—but a romantic relationship isn't one of them. The fact is, you want a boyfriend for the wrong reasons, whether it's to keep up with your friends or to give you an insta-social life. What you'd actually find is that although you get all that stuff in a relationship, you'd also have to spend hours talking through problems and sacrifice some time with your girlfriends. And right now that's just not something you want to do. That's cool. Save yourself (and a boy) relationship stuff until you're ready.

IF YOU SCORED 35 TO 60: **Definitely Datable**

Confidence? Check. Spare time? Check. A commitment to working through probs? Um, well . . . Okay, so you're on your way to becoming relationship ready. But a few questions pulled down your score, which means that you shouldn't dive into the deep end just yet. Think of it like this: When you're a freshman, you usually don't get picked as a starter on the varsity girls' basketball team. You need practice. So right now consider yourself on the junior-varsity team—dating around, learning the moves that'll help you be a natural when it comes to a big relationship. Continue your casual dating and you'll learn the basics, from getting through little fights to figuring out how to budget time between your boy and your buds.

IF YOU SCORED 65 TO 90: **Ready for Romance**

How'd you get to be such a relationship expert? Probably through lots of firsthand experience. You know that dating a guy because he's a Matt Damon clone won't be enough glue to hold a full-fledged relationship together. You have to actually like the guy and be capable of letting him get to know you. Because even though it's fun to do group dates at Pizza Hut or romantic movies alone together, when the date's over, you're still his girlfriend—and that means sticking around even when the going gets tough. But why are we telling you this? For a relationship pro like you, this is basic stuff.

Seven Clues Your Crush Isn't Interested

* He constantly mentions what a great friend you are.
* You only get a form letter back from his fan club.
* He tells you—in detail—about how delicious Drew Barrymore is.
* He begs you to hook him up with your hot friend.
* It turns out that the restraining order he handed you was not a joke.
* You asked him out, and he said no.
* When you call your crush's house, his brother always tells you he isn't there. (Then you find out that he doesn't even have a brother.)

6. What kind of girlfriend would you be?

Okay, so you know you're ready for major-league love—a serious relationship. But do you have any idea what you'd be like as a girlfriend? This quiz will reveal the truth.

1. If your boyfriend were to talk to his ex-girlfriend on the phone for an hour, you'd be angry.
True: Go to 2   *False: Go to 3*

2. The guy should always pay for the date.
True: Go to 4   *False: Go to 5*

3. If your boyfriend couldn't make it to the school dance because of a family emergency, you'd go anyway.
True: Go to 6   *False: Go to 5*

4. You'd expect your boyfriend to be up on all the gossip about your friends.
True: Go to 7   *False: Go to 8*

5. If he forgot your one-month anniversary, he would be in big trouble.
True: Go to 7   *False: Go to 8*

6. If you and your best friend got in a fight, you'd go into all the details with your boyfriend.
True: Go to 8   *False: Go to 9*

7. When your boyfriend buys holiday presents, you expect the most expensive gift he buys to be yours.
True: Go to 10   *False: Go to 11*

8. For your grandparents' fiftieth anniversary, your family throws a major shindig. You'd assume your boyfriend would come and hang for the entire night.
True: Go to 11   *False: Go to 12*

9. You really dislike that whole public-display-of-affection thing.
True: Go to 12   *False: Go to 11*

10. You're turned off by guys who don't open doors for you.
True: Go to Spoil-Me Sweetie *False: Go to 13*

11. You love using the word *boyfriend* and being called somebody's girlfriend.
True: Go to 13 *False: Go to Hands-Off Honey*

12. Your guy gets a scholarship to soccer camp for the summer. You'd like to have the option of seeing other guys since he'll be gone for so long.
True: Go to Hands-Off Honey *False: Go to Give-and-Take Girl*

13. If your boyfriend was in a rotten mood around you, you wouldn't take it personally.
True: Go to Give-and-Take Girl *False: Go to Spoil-Me Sweetie*

SCORING

Spoil-Me Sweetie

Most likely to: Be pampered like a princess by your boy.
What drives guys crazy (in a good way) about you: You're so picky that he feels very special when you reveal that you like him. Plus you expect him to be a total gentleman—which he kind of enjoys but would die of embarrassment if his friends knew.
What drives guys crazy (in a bad way) about you: Fight much? Thought so. With high standards like yours, it seems like you and your guy are always having little spats.

Be kind to your boy by: Returning the favor and spoiling him every once in a while. Whether it's a sweet love note, a homemade mix tape, or a dinner-and-a-movie night (on you!), a little generosity on your part will let him know you appreciate all his hard work.

Give-and-Take Girl

Most likely to: Stay friends after a breakup.

What drives guys crazy (in a good way) about you: Just when he thinks you can't get any cooler, you prove him wrong by understanding his cranky mood or actually suggesting going to that gross horror movie he's dying to see.

What drives guys crazy (in a bad way) about you: You've got the game of love down so well that sometimes you make him feel clueless.

Be kind to your boy by: Keeping your mushiest moments on the down low, especially when you're around his friends. On top of being a cool, nonclingy-girlfriend move, it makes you appear ultraconfident—like you don't depend on your boyfriend for your identity.

Hands-Off Honey

Most likely to: Not be devastated if a relationship doesn't work out.

What drives guys crazy (in a good way) about you: The cat-and-mouse chasing game never really ends. Since you're so busy with your own stuff, potential boyfriends have to keep working at getting to know your mysterious self.

What drives guys crazy (in a bad way) about you: You're so incredibly private that guys you date may have a hard time getting to know the real you. And they rarely get a sense of how much you like them, so they may eventually get tired of chasing.

Be kind to your boy by: Letting him into your head, especially when you need some sound advice. It lets him know that you respect his intelligence—and that there is a heart under that cool facade of yours.

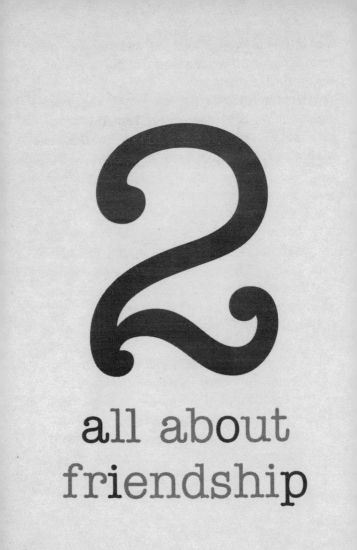

2

all about
friendship

life would be really lame without friends. After all, who would laugh at your jokes? Pick you up when you're bummed? Tell you gently that you should never, ever wear those capri pants again? Yep—true friends can make the world a much brighter place. But what kind of friends would make your world perfect? And how do you treat the ones you have? The quizzes in this chapter will help you figure out your perfect friend type and clue you in to where you belong in your social universe. And oh yeah—since even you might not be 100 percent flaw-free (gasp! the horror!), we'll also test out your friendship skills to see if you're worthy of their worship.

1. What's your friendship style?

When it comes to your nearest and dearest, do you prefer a small few or a huge posse? Find out if you're a group groupie with these questions.

1. You win a $500 gift certificate to a really fancy beauty salon. The only catch: You have to use it all in one day. How do you splurge?

(a) Get the full, deluxe beauty treatment—manicure, pedicure, hair highlights, professional makeup.

(b) Take two close friends with you and get a round of haircuts, pro makeup, and manicures.

(c) Take twenty friends and treat everyone to manicures.

2. You rush to your locker between classes, and when you open the door, you see a rose. There's a little note attached—from your secret admirer! Within the hour who knows about this sweet surprise?

(a) Just you and your admirer.

(b) A friend or two in your class. Something this cool, you can't keep totally hush-hush.

(c) Your entire class, since you bring the rose along and spill the story to each person who walks in the room.

3. On Saturday morning you wake up with a major case of the blues. It's so bad that you barely want to get out of bed. How do you deal?

(a) Stay under the sheets with a book or the TV remote and wait for the stinky mood to pass.

(b) Call your best friend and tell her you need some serious cheering up. She'll come to your rescue.

(c) Organize a group trip to the mall, because being surrounded by people always puts you in a better state of mind.

4. If you were to run for student government, what kind of strategy would you most likely use—aside from writing an awesome speech to read at the school assembly?

(a) Put up tons of posters that state what you'd do as class officer.

(b) Have a few friends help hand out lollipops with your cool-but-relevant campaign slogan on them.

(c) Throw a campaign party at your house.

5. Which of the following descriptions sounds most like your address book?

(a) Some relatives plus a couple of friends you've known since you were little but rarely call.

(b) A few names and numbers, and you call all of them frequently.

(c) Almost all of the pages are full, and you can barely remember a few names in there.

6. A best-friends-forever necklace charm is . . .

(a) a really serious thing—something you'd give to only one person.

(b) a sweet way to let your friend know that you've felt really close to her lately.

(c) a bit of a problem for you unless they make one that comes in, like, twenty pieces.

Count up the number of times you selected each letter, then read the answer section for that letter below.

Number of A's ▨   *Number of B's* ▨   *Number of C's* ▨

IF YOU CHOSE MOSTLY A'S: **Searching for a Soul Mate**

You're pretty careful when it comes to opening up to people. Most of your top secret, personal info stays locked inside that head of yours. Spending time alone is something you really groove on, and you pride yourself on the fact that you rarely have to ask anyone for favors.

Others probably see you as serious and maybe a little shy, but you see yourself as someone who's just waiting for the right friend. But here's the problemo, amiga: The current status of your social life doesn't leave you with many chances to find that person. In order to meet new people, you may have to consider putting yourself out there, because right now your vibe is saying, "Leave me alone!" Start small. Is there a girl in your classes or your neighborhood who's always been friendly to you? Ask if she wants to hang out after school and do homework together or maybe even rent a movie. And don't be disappointed if friendship doesn't blossom overnight. It takes time to build a great relationship—but it's definitely worth the wait.

IF YOU CHOSE MOSTLY B'S: **Keeping It Small**

You like to trust a small group of friends with your heart

and your secrets. When you go out, it's almost always with the same cool buds you love—and you know almost everything about one another.

When people see you without a certain friend, do they automatically wonder where she is? That's because they think of you as part of a tight little circle. When you're together, everyone notices because you never stop talking or laughing. And since you seem like so much fun, there are probably a lot of people in your life who'd like to get to know you a little better.

Make sure that you leave room for new friends. Yes, it's important to stay close with your best buds, but they don't have to make up your entire universe. You can (and should) have friendships with other people; that's how you learn new things and build confidence—plus it'll keep you from being glued to your closest friends.

IF YOU CHOSE MOSTLY C'S: **The More the Merrier**
In your opinion, there is no such thing as having too many friends—and that's a cool philosophy to have. When you're in a massive group like yours, there's rarely a dull moment—someone's always got a crisis or a funny story or a great idea for something fun to do. And since you have so many friends to pick from, there's always somebody to hang with and something to talk about, so the boredom factor is, like, less than zero.

However, unless you make a special effort to stand out as an individual, people may assume that you have enough friends already and that you don't need one more. To bust this myth, you need to be extra friendly when you meet someone you'd like to get to know better. Another bummer about group friendships is that lots of the bonding is just surface-level stuff: jokes, parties, movies, whatever. For serious heart-to-hearts, you need the special trust and closeness of a one-on-one friendship. So is there anyone you can go to when tough times come around? If not, pick someone out of your larger group, since everyone can't be your confidante.

2. Are you fun to hang with?

Love being the life of the party? Or are you more the type to blend in with the wallpaper? Discover how to improve your social style with this quiz.

1. If you were totally underdressed for a party, would you leave?
Yes: *Go to 2*   **No:** *Go to 3*

2. At a party, do you talk to almost every guest by the end of the night?
Yes: *Go to 4*   **No:** *Go to 5*

3. Do people often say you're too sensitive?
Yes: *Go to 6*   **No:** *Go to 5*

4. Do you almost always remember people's names?
Yes: *Go to 7*   **No:** *Go to 8*

5. Are you uncomfortable striking up conversations with strangers?
Yes: *Go to 9*   **No:** *Go to 7*

6. Do you often complain about not feeling well?
Yes: *Go to 9*   **No:** *Go to 8*

7. Are you frequently the first one out on the dance floor?
Yes: Go to 10   **No:** Go to 11

8. Do you often run out of things to talk about?
Yes: Go to 12   **No:** Go to 10

9. Do you tend to forget the punch lines to jokes?
Yes: Go to 12   **No:** Go to 11

10. Do you love pulling practical jokes on people?
Yes: Go to Permanent Party   **No:** Go to Life of the Party

11. Do you live for meeting new people?
Yes: Go to Life of the Party   **No:** Go to Party of One

12. When someone asks what you want to do, do you often say, "I dunno"?
Yes: Go to Party of One   **No:** Go to 11

SCORING

Permanent Party

Sounds like you're a blast to hang with—always coming up with fresh ideas for cool things to do. Another fun thing about you: You've got zero fear of embarrassment. You love it when all eyes are on you as people wait to be entertained. But . . . watch out for hogging the spotlight too much; there are some times when you'll have to be serious. Also, sensitive people may not dig being the butt of your jokes. Don't forget to play nice!

Life of the Party

Like the oh-so-yummy Snickers bar, you're the perfect combination of nutty and sweet. You've got the social-grace thing mastered—you crack up your friends without crossing the line and being obnoxious. Boredom doesn't last long with you. As soon as it hits, you kick into gear and think of something entertaining to do. Sometimes you shy away from what sounds like a good time because you're worried about how you'll look. That kind of thinking may hold you back from doing some pretty fun stuff. Follow your gut, not your friends.

Party of One
You'd rather be the audience than the star, safely watching the fun without taking chances. That way you're pretty much guaranteed no embarrassment—but isn't that kind of boring? You end up hanging out where your friends want to go (but not necessarily where you're happiest!), and since you're a little shy around people you don't know, there's not much of a chance for you to make new friends. To boost your fun factor, learn a few good jokes (and practice telling them) or start reading lots of magazines, which will give you new topics to talk about.

You Know Your Social Life's Ready for a Makeover When . . .

* You can recite the names of all the Teletubbies.
* You are so lovin' *Baywatch* reruns, and you think David Hasselhoff is underappreciated as an actor.
* You spend Saturday night in your closet, rearranging your shoes. And naming them.
* You call your best friend and say, "Hey, it's me," and there's dead silence—until you say your name . . . first and last name.

* You fix your hair and makeup before heading outside to get the mail from the mailbox.
* You don't know how to answer when someone asks, "What's up?"

3. Do you groove on gossip?

Sure, it's fun to know the inside scoop on your best friends. But are you more in the loop than, like, the <u>National Enquirer</u>? Find out if you're addicted to gossip by answering these questions.

1. You stop in the bathroom before class to do a quickie lipstick check. A girl you kinda-sorta know barges in, crying. When you ask if she's okay, she says she just got dumped by her boyfriend (who just happens to be your best friend's crush)—then she swears you to secrecy. Your move?

  (a) Tell no one—word will get out quick enough.
  (b) Tell only your best friend and swear her to secrecy.
  (c) Tell a few select friends but make them promise to keep it on the down low.

2. You hear from a few sources that the new girl in class is a witch. Not the whoa-that-girl-is-mean kind—we're talkin' the freaky, black-magic kind. (You did notice that she wears a lot of black. . . .) When you get partnered with her for a science experiment, how do you cope?

  (a) You introduce yourself and let her make her own first impression.

(b) You're nice and friendly, but you keep an eye peeled for any weird, witchy moves.

(c) You whisper, "Help!" in your friend's ear and ask to be partnered with her instead.

3. When you like a guy, which of the following sounds most like your boy-getting strategy?

(a) You talk to him and send major flirty vibes his way.

(b) You flirt a little and send a friend on a fact-finding mission, or you hint at your feelings when one of his friends is within earshot.

(c) You let your secret "slip" to a bunch of friends and expect the grapevine to be your cupid.

4. Good friends share their secrets with you and/or let you read their diaries

(a) all the time.

(b) every once in a while.

(c) pretty rarely.

5. Your English teacher is seriously annoyed. It turns out that someone stole a copy of the final exam, so the new version will be much harder—unless the thief confesses. When you hear a rumor about who stole the test, what do you do?

(a) Blow it off. There's no proof.

(b) Hint (loudly) around the guy that you really, really would like to pass English this year. Hopefully he'll get it.

(c) Slip an anonymous note to the teacher that tells her what you've heard.

Count up the number of times you selected each letter, then read the answer section next to the letter you selected most often.

IF YOU SELECTED MOSTLY A'S: **Minding Your Own Business**

Major applause for you, girlfriend. You manage to fight the gossip addiction and let people make their own impressions on you. Sometimes you may feel pretty clueless, especially when it comes to knowing who's dating whom. But a bonus about being you is that people trust you with their secrets—you've proven yourself as someone who can keep her mouth shut, and that trust is a key ingredient in building friendships. Just make sure that you demand the same level of respect from the friends you spill your guts to.

IF YOU SELECTED MOSTLY B'S: **Tuned in to the Grapevine**

The good news is, you're like 90 percent of the people at your school when it comes to gossip. You like to get the inside scoop, but you would never dream of adding to it. The bad news? You still can't say no to that naughty little pleasure, even though you know you should. By tuning in to the school grapevine, you give gossip addicts a captive audience. And in case you haven't found out the hard way, someday you might end up the target of those nasty rumors. Stop contributing to the cycle now, and you'll save yourself some big-time ouches later on.

4. Are you a good listener?

Do friends turn to you when they need a shoulder to cry on? Or is a convo with you more like a never-ending episode of The Me Show? This quiz will reveal how in tune your ears are.

1. You would describe yourself as very talkative.
True/False

2. If your friend gets in a fight with her boyfriend, it's okay to call him a jerk. *True/False*

3. You always know what to buy people for their birthdays because you remember little hints they dropped throughout the year. *True/False*

4. You have a really short attention span. *True/False*

5. If your friend called with a problem during your favorite show, you would listen while keeping your eyes glued to the TV. *True/False*

6. Your parents often have to remind you to do your chores. *True/False*

7. You have a great memory. *True/False*

8. People sometimes complain that you interrupt too often. *True/False*

9. Your friend who's superskinny says she thinks she's fat. A good listener should say, "That's stupid— you're so skinny!" *True/False*

10. You can usually come up with advice within sixty seconds of listening to somebody talk. *True/False*

11. You always wait to be asked for advice instead of just offering it. *True/False*

12. When you meet someone new, you always ask more questions than you answer. *True/False*

13. When two of your friends are fighting, you like to hear both sides so you can sort out the fight instead of staying out of it. *True/False*

14. You take great notes when teachers lecture in class. *True/False*

15. Sometimes you forget people's names. *True/False*

16. You can always sense when someone isn't telling the truth. *True/False*

SCORING

Add up your points using the answer key below, then read the corresponding paragraph that follows to rate your listening skills.

1. True = 5, false = 0

2. True = 5, false = 0

3. True = 0, false = 5

4. True = 5, false = 0

5. True = 5, false = 0	**11.** True = 0, false = 5
6. True = 5, false = 0	**12.** True = 0, false = 5
7. True = 0, false = 5	**13.** True = 5, false = 0
8. True = 5, false = 0	**14.** True = 0, false = 5
9. True = 5, false = 0	**15.** True = 5, false = 0
10. True = 5, false = 0	**16.** True = 0, false = 5

IF YOU SCORED 0 TO 20: **I'm All Ears**

You don't just listen well; you sense well. That means you hear what people say, but you also tune in to their body language—do they seem uncomfortable? Angry? In need of some serious cheering up? You can sniff out the mood and ask the right questions to get people to open up. Plus you're totally prepared to give up a big chunk of time while someone spills the problem, which means that any advice you give will be superthoughtful. People love crying on your shoulder because once they're finished, you've erased their bad moods. Ever consider a career as a counselor, a judge . . . or a quiz-book writer? With ears like yours, you'd be a natural.

IF YOU SCORED 25 TO 50: **I Can Sorta Hear You**

You get points for wanting to be a good listener. And it looks like you have some of the key ingredients, like a commitment to helping people make the right decisions. But the problem is that sometimes when a friend is pouring her heart out, you're only half listening, which means you can't give good advice. To add some muscle to your listening powers, remove all distractions when a friend needs you to listen. Turn off the TV or (if you're face-to-face) make eye contact. Your friend will feel like you're much more interested—and (bonus!) she'll be happy to listen next time you have a prob.

IF YOU SCORED 55 TO 80: **Did You Say Something?** You don't like to dwell on the same subject for too long—and it drives you nuts when friends complain about a problem but never do anything to fix it. These qualities make it kind of tough for you to be a good listener. When a friend's in need, you listen to a quick version and then give her your solution—and that's the end of it. But here's a secret: Your friends may feel like you're blowing them off. Sometimes what people need isn't a quick fix, but just some time to vent their feelings. Yeah, it takes longer, but by letting your friends cry on your shoulder, you're showing them that you really care—and that you'll stick around until they feel better.

5. Do you fight fair?

When there's a major blowup, do you lose your head? Or can you handle even the most ugly situations without losing your cool?

1. Do you often raise your voice when you argue?
   Yes: Go to 2   *No: Go to 3*
2. When you fight, do you sometimes say things that you don't mean?
   Yes: Go to 4   *No: Go to 5*
3. When you're mad, do you shut down and avoid the situation?
   Yes: Go to 5   *No: Go to 6*

4. When it comes to making up, do you usually wait for the other person to make the first move?
Yes: Go to 7   *No: Go to 8*

5. If you're in a bad mood, do you sometimes snap at people around you?
Yes: Go to 7   *No: Go to 9*

6. If your friend does something that hurts you, do you mention it at the moment?
Yes: Go to 9   *No: Go to 8*

7. In a big fight, do you bring up old issues that you're still mad about?
Yes: Go to 10   *No: Go to 11*

8. Do you and your friends refuse to speak to one another when you're fighting?
Yes: Go to 7   *No: Go to 9*

9. If you and your best friend have an argument, do you tell other friends all about it?
Yes: Go to 11   *No: Go to 12*

10. Do you point and gesture wildly or really get in someone's face when you fight?
Yes: Go to Five-Alarm Fighter   *No: Go to 11*

11. When you argue, do you often call the other person nasty names to her face?
Yes: Go to Five-Alarm Fighter   *No: Go to Totally Tough Cookie*

12. Do you usually walk away from an argument with everything fixed and everyone happy again?
Yes: Go to Red-Hot Referee   *No: Go to Totally Tough Cookie*

Five-Alarm Fighter

Your fighting style: The loudest person wins.

Your weapons: Sharp words, intimidating body language, and a major refusal to back down from an argument.

The boo-boos you walk away with: Sometimes even you don't recognize that red-faced, furious girl you become when you're angry. You might have lost some friends as a result of things you said but didn't mean. And you've also developed a reputation of being a girl with a bad temper.

Try this tactic: Sounds like you just get wrapped up in your emotions when you fight. Next time you feel like you're getting out of control, put off the argument while you cool off. (Say, "Can we talk about this later, once I've had time to think it over?") Then you can go home and scream into your pillow—and discuss the issue calmly once you've chilled.

Totally Tough Cookie

Your fighting style: The one with the most people on her side wins.

Your weapons: Your face-to-face face-off style, which never crosses the line into cruelty. Plus your friends, who get wrapped up in all your fights.

The boo-boos you walk away with: When you turn private disagreements into public knowledge, the person you're fighting with could get even more overheated. It's a form of trust breaking, which is especially bad to do when your friendship is already in such a delicate state.

Try this tactic: First, don't let your anger build up to the exploding point. If you have a problem with your friend, try to talk it out calmly, using the words, "I felt hurt when . . ." instead of accusing her with, "You always . . ." Next, keep your trap shut publicly when you're in a fight. If you need a second opinion, go to someone who's out of the social loop, like a parent.

Red-Hot Referee

Your fighting style: Nobody wins unless the fight is settled.

Your weapons: A major dose of patience and great listening skills.

The boo-boos you walk away with: Usually you avoid major blowups altogether, but sometimes it's unavoidable. Luckily your cooler-than-cool problem-solving skills and ability to not totally freak out when you're mad allow you to handle things without causing major damage. However, you may have a tough time realizing that not everybody has this fighting style. The person you're battling may be a screamer or an avoider, and that means you'll have to be extra patient as you deal with them. Plus be careful not to take it too personally if they lose it with you— remember that they just can't deal with arguments as well as you can.

Try this tactic: When you find yourself in a virtually unfixable fight, here's something you can try: Put yourself in the other person's shoes. (Um, not literally.) Look at the argument from her side and see if the problem becomes more clear.

6. How far would you go to be popular?

Everybody likes being liked. But when you let popularity rule your life, you could find yourself with faux friends. Take this quiz to find out if you're a clique-aholic.

1. The yummy basketball captain asked you to the movies. When the lights go down in the theater, he's all over you like static cling. What's your move?

> *(a) Call, "Time-out!" and tell him if he doesn't knock it off, you're going home. You don't care what kind of rumors he'll spread at school.*
>
> *(b) Play along until he gets too touchy, then gently ask him to stop. You don't want to seem like a total prude in front of such a popular guy.*
>
> *(c) Jump in and play ball, even though your head is saying no. Otherwise he might not ask you out again and you can forget about being on the prom court.*

2. A bunch of popular people you'd love to be friends with just invited you to a Midnight Madness party. The prob? Your curfew is eleven P.M. When one of the girls offers to pick you up, you say:

> *(a) "I'd love to go, but my parents would kill me. Catch ya next time."*
>
> *(b) "Ugh—I have to work tonight, and I don't get off until one. Maybe I'll try to swing by afterward."*
>
> *(c) "Cool—I'll meet you on the next block once I sneak out."*

3. There's a new girl at school—she just moved from New York, and she seems totally different. You'd like to get tight with her before the class royalty lures her into their circle. So when she asks to copy your answers during your history test, you

(a) say no—then immediately change your mind about her coolness factor.

(b) pretend to be totally in the test zone and act like you don't hear her.

(c) slide your test to the edge of the desk and give her a sly smile.

4. Lucky day! You end up in the cafeteria line behind the group of girls you've always thought seemed amazingly cool. While you're waiting in line to pay for some gross, foam-like pizza, you see the cashier drop a roll of pennies, which explodes all over the floor. The girls in front of you crack up and start making fun of the cashier. You

(a) stoop down and help the cashier pick up the pennies.

(b) suddenly become very interested in your pizza and ignore them.

(c) laugh and try to come up with something funny to say to the girls in front of you.

5. You've made it—one of the girls from the cool crowd invites you to a big party. When you get there, you're even more psyched to spot a bunch of cuties from the local college. One of them comes over to chat, then he hands you a beer. You're not into drinking, but here's this babe handing you a can—in front of all these superimportant people. How do you cope?

(a) Hand it back and tell him you don't drink.

(b) Take the can and hold it but never take a sip.

c) Pop it open and drink so you don't look like a baby.

SCORING

Count up the number of times you selected each letter, then read the answer section below the letter you selected most.

IF YOU SELECTED MOSTLY A'S: **Peer Pressure –Proof**
You don't respect people just because they're popular. With you they have to earn it, so you'll never stray down the wrong path on the journey to popularity. Chances are, you're known for your originality, and people aren't surprised when you don't follow the group. In fact, you're probably secretly admired by others who aren't as comfy speaking up for themselves. In other words, could you be any cooler?

IF YOU SELECTED MOSTLY B'S: **Avoiding the Issue**
You stick to your morals, no matter how intense the pressure gets. The problem is, in your quest for popularity you often hide behind little white lies. When you pretend not to see a problem or blame your decision on something out of your control ("I can't smoke because I have asthma. . . .") instead of just saying no, you lose an opportunity to gain respect. Think about it: Do you want the kind of friends you have to lie to 24/7? If you have to hide the real you, they aren't real friends.

IF YOU SELECTED MOSTLY C'S: **Follow the Leader**

IF YOU SELECTED MOSTLY C'S: **Follow the Leader**
Sure, you know the difference between right and wrong—but that doesn't mean you do the right thing all the time. In fact, there have been times lately when you've chosen the wrong path because you thought it would make you seem cooler to certain people. But the friends that you make this way are only temporary. The truth is, you have to respect yourself before you can get respect from others. And by going along with the crowd, you're disrespecting yourself every day. To start rebuilding your self-image, go through the questions above and read the A answers, then try to model your behavior after them.

7. Can your friends trust you?

It's the main ingredient in strong friendships— trust. So are you more dependable than an Energizer battery or less reliable than a weather forecast? Find out with this quiz.

DIRECTIONS: Grade each of the following statements with a **1** (if it's totally unlike you), **2** (if it's sort of like you), or **3** (if it's so like you, it's scary).

1. You hardly ever cancel plans at the last minute when you don't feel like going out.

2. If someone leaves a message, you never forget to call back.

3. You wouldn't try to avoid a friend because she's in a bad mood.

4. You always write back when people send you letters or e-mails.

5. When your friend is really stressed about a test or assignment, you remember to ask how it went.

6. You have never, ever forgotten a friend's birthday.

7. Friends' ex-boyfriends and crushes are off-limits unless you ask your friend's permission before you make a move.

8. You never talk about your friends behind their backs. (Be honest!)

9. When you borrow something (a CD, a shirt, whatever) from a friend, you always return it before they ask.

10. If you were at a friend's house and found her diary, you wouldn't even dream of peeking inside.

11. If you accidentally broke your friend's sunglasses, then fixed them with Krazy Glue, you would still tell her and offer to pay for new ones.

12. You have never asked a friend to lie for you.

13. When you're in a fight with a friend, you still keep her secrets locked up tight.

14. If your friend wasn't allowed out this weekend until her room was clean, you would go over and help—even if it takes all day Saturday and Sunday.

15. You often surprise your friends with little treats, like homemade cookies.

Add up the numbers you wrote in the blanks, then read your answer section below.

IF YOU SCORED 15 TO 25: **Flaky as Pop-Tarts**

Sorry to break the harsh news to you, but your buds probably don't feel like they can lean on you. When the day comes that you need a friend, you might look around and realize you're all alone. Boost your dependability by starting with the small stuff—remembering birthdays, calling friends back as soon as you get their messages. Once friends start to feel your warmth, they'll come back around.

IF YOU SCORED 26 TO 34: **Bubble Yum Good**

You meet all the basic friendship rules—you're trustworthy and rarely flake out on anyone. And although you can't be there for all your friends 100 percent of the time, there are one or two extra-special people who you will go out of your way for. Just remember: Don't take a close friendship for granted. Best buds don't come with guarantees.

IF YOU SCORED 35 TO 45: **The Everlasting Gobstopper**

You're the ultimate friend-till-the-end—and your buds consider themselves lucky to have you. Whether it's just hanging out or having a serious heart-to-heart, you play a majorly active role in your friends' lives. Just one pointer: Pay attention to whether your friends are this good to you, too. If you're doing all the giving and getting nothing in return, you're selling yourself short big time.

all about the
inner you

nah—we're not talking about spleens and kidneys. The quizzes in this chapter are all about deep stuff like your mind, your moods, and your emotions—all the complex layers that create your personality. Caution: You might notice that your answers change more quickly than you change socks. That's cool; freak not. Your personality is a constant work in progress, shifting a little every day. Your answers today will help reveal the inner you of the moment—and maybe show you the next direction you'll want to grow in. Plus you'll find proven methods you can use to start improving what you don't like!

1. How outgoing are you?

Do you feel okay doing the meet-and-greet thing with new people? Or do you take a while to warm up to potential pals? Find out your shyness factor with this quiz.

1. Whoa—drool alert! The deejay at your friend's Sweet 16 is a separated-at-birth twin of David Boreanaz, and you think he maybe-sorta-kinda just smiled at you. What's your next step?

    (a) Ask him if he's allowed to slow dance on the job.
    (b) Go up to him and request a song.
    (c) Get your friend to keep an eye on him as you walk by to see if he watches you.

2. You're having lunch with your mom at the mall food court when you see a teacher from school. She's pushing a stroller with a way cute baby in it. What do you do?

    (a) Run up and say hi, then ask to hold the baby.
    (b) Wave and if she comes over, introduce your mom.
    (c) Hide—you see enough of each other at school.

3. It's the last day of school. And okay, since you never got around to revealing your love to your crush, today's your final chance to chat him up. With your yearbook in hand, you would most likely

    (a) walk over and say, "Hey, you didn't sign mine yet." Then when you sign his, write your phone number and "Call me!" inside.

(b) casually walk over and say something harmless yet friendly, like, "So, what are you up to this summer?"
(c) stare at him from afar and draw hearts around his photo in your yearbook.

4. At the drugstore you spot a lady wearing the exact shade of red nail polish (not too orange, not too fire-engine) you've searched the globe for. What's your move?

(a) Grab her hand and say, "I have to know where you got that nail polish!"
(b) Try to run into her at the cash register and say, "Excuse me, I love your nail polish. Where did you get it?"
(c) Head over to the cosmetics aisle and start searching in hopes that she bought it at this store.

5. You order a bacon cheeseburger well done, but when the waitress delivers it to the table, it looks so pink, you think it might moo. As she starts to leave, what do you do?

(a) Yell, "Wait a second! This isn't what I ordered." You'd expect an apology.
(b) Say, "Excuse me, but I asked for well done," and send it back for more cooking.
(c) Start munching on the fries and the cheesy bacon but leave the burger to die in peace.

SCORING

Add up the number of times you selected each letter, then read the scoring section for the letter you selected most.

IF YOU SELECTED MOSTLY A'S: **In Your Face**

Nobody would ever accuse you of being shy. In fact, in your quest to be friendly, you often cross the line of politeness. And sometimes it works to your advantage—like, with guys—because you aren't afraid to ask for what you want! However, mellow out that bulldozer attitude, especially when you're dealing with strangers and adults. A little "please" and "thank you" can make you appear mucho mature-o—and get you better results.

IF YOU SELECTED MOSTLY B'S: **In Sync**

Most of the time you're able to function just fine in the friendliness department. But when it comes to situations involving potential embarrassment—particularly in front of somebody with dreamy eyes and dimples—you really have to force yourself to be outgoing. So do it—because each time you overcome a shyness-inducing sitch by faking confidence, you actually get more confident. Neat trick, right? Keep pushing yourself bit by bit, and soon you'll be schmoozing like a natural!

IF YOU SELECTED MOSTLY C'S: **In My Shell**

Come out, come out, wherever you are! You're so busy hiding in your hole that you're missing out on some pretty cool stuff, like, well, life. When you think about taking a chance and getting to know new people, you're overcome by fear. Think people will laugh at you? Or find you boring? We'll let you in on a little secret: Everybody has those fears about themselves, and the best way to get to know new people is by easing their fears. Ask questions about what they like to do or compliment them on something. Make them feel special and interesting, and they'll think you're pretty awesome. Still not convinced? Check out the sidebar below for more shyness-busting tips.

How to Conquer Shyness

✳ *Learn Bold Body Language*
Although it might feel awkward at first, here are some body lingo clues that are guaranteed to make you look outgoing: Keep your chin up, make eye contact, hold your shoulders back, and flash a big smile. Train yourself to master these signals, and after a while you'll carry yourself like a pro 24/7.

✳ *Turn Up the Voice Volume*
Don't mutter or whisper just because it's hard to get out the words. Speak loudly and clearly, being careful not to let your words run together.

✳ *Play 20 Questions*
Ask people about everything that comes to mind—that way you're talking without having the pressure of the spotlight on you.

✳ *Always Have a Challenge for Yourself*
Whether it's to say hi to five people in the hall every day or to figure out a way to have a full-on conversation with your crush, set a goal and go for it.

2. Are you happy?

Do school, friends, and family make your world a brighter place to be, or are you constantly wallowing in the blues? Find out how content you are by answering these Q's.

DIRECTIONS: Grade each of the following statements with a **1** (if it's totally unlike you), **2** (if it's sort of like you), or **3** (if it's so like you, it's scary).

1. You never get jealous.

2. You frequently laugh so hard that tears run down your face.

3. Most of your friends are cheerful people.

4. There are lots of things you can't wait to do every day.

5. You often pat yourself on the back for a job well done.

6. When something bad happens, you have a few good friends who always help you out.

7. You don't like to gossip.

8. You love to try new games, sports, and hobbies.

9. When you feel stressed, you take a time-out to relax.

10. On the first day of school you're more excited than scared.

11. Overall, you have a good relationship with your family.

12. You frequently think of yourself as a lucky person.

13. You don't get upset very easily.

14. When a friend is in a bad mood, you don't take it personally.

15. You like the way you look.

SCORING

Add up the numbers you wrote in the blanks and read your answer section below.

IF YOU SCORED 15 TO 25: **Blue You**

What's with the gloomy 'tude? It seems like there are few things going on in your life right now that bring you joy. Try keeping a mood journal and see if you can notice patterns—what makes you most frustrated? Is it a certain friend? A hard class? By focusing on the problem, you may be able to cure it—and move a step closer to happiness. One warning: If you feel constantly down and nothing helps, speak to an adult you can trust—a parent, family friend, or school counselor. You don't have to deal with those feelings alone!

IF YOU SCORED 26 TO 35: **Sunshine Yellow**

Sure, there are days when you'll just be bummed from the moment you roll out of bed—but most of the time you've got a pretty good attitude about your life. But wouldn't you like to be blissed out more often? (We all would!) There's an easy way to help make that happen. Start by figuring out what makes you really happy. Eliminate downer friends from your crew and spend more time with people who make you feel great. Also, invest more time in activities that make you happy, whether it's walking your dog or dancing around your bedroom. You should be on your way to full-fledged happiness in no time!

IF YOU SCORED 36 TO 45: **Tickled Pink**
You have such a positive attitude—if you could bottle this emotion, you'd be a bazillionaire. Thanks to your optimistic outlook, even the crummiest of days become bearable. And friends love the fact that you never fail to cheer them up and help them realize that their problems aren't the end of the world. Just be sure that you aren't afraid to deal with life's unhappy moments. Sometimes the best cure for serious sadness is crying on a friend's shoulder instead of faking a smile.

3. How confident are you?

You're fun, funny, and fabulous—but do you believe it? To find out whether your self-esteem needs a big ole boost, answer these questions.

1. You find it easy to talk to strangers—at school, at the 7-Eleven, at parties.
True: Go to 2   *False: Go to 3*

2. You believe that people are born confident.
True: Go to 4   *False: Go to 5*

3. You would never say anything that could be interpreted as bragging.
True: Go to 6   *False: Go to 5*

4. You can make great things happen just by believing in them.
True: *Go to 7*   ***False:*** *Go to 8*

5. You could make small talk with Madonna if she showed up at your friend's party.
True: *Go to 7*   ***False:*** *Go to 9*

6. You have at least one friend who brings you down.
True: *Go to 9*   ***False:*** *Go to 8*

7. Sometimes you might come off as being arrogant.
True: *Go to Cocky Chica*   ***False:*** *Go to Secure Sister*

8. When someone compliments your hair, you usually brush it off with an "oh no—it looks terrible today."
True: *Go to Downer Dame*   ***False:*** *Go to 7*

9. People often think you're shy.
True: *Go to Downer Dame*   ***False:*** *Go to Secure Sister*

SCORING

Cocky Chica

Having rock-solid confidence is great—it means you believe in yourself and ensures that you'll go far in life. However, don't buy into the hype so much that you think you don't have to work as hard. It's great to know that you're smart, for example, but that doesn't mean you shouldn't do your homework or study for a test. Always make an effort to improve yourself—even if you were great to start with!

Secure Sister

With this balance of confidence and grace, you're golden.

You're secure enough to believe in yourself, and that helps you in all areas of your life—school, friendships, sports, love. You know you deserve the best, and you won't settle for less. However, you're also respectful of people's feelings, so you don't like to rub your success in their faces. That's sweet. Just continue to accept praise graciously, and generously hand it out sometimes, too.

Downer Dame

If there were a fan club for you, you wouldn't want to be a member. You sabotage yourself by deflecting compliments and staying friends with people who drag you down. Maybe it's just because you have high standards; you think that you should never stop trying to improve yourself. That's great. But you can continue to better yourself without beating yourself up. Take a giant step in the confidence department by accepting compliments with a simple "thanks" and a smile. Soon all that good thinking will sink in.

Seven Self-Esteem-Busting Phrases to Vacate from Your Vocab

* I'm so fat.
* I wish I had her hair/style/eyes/whatever.
* I'm not good enough.
* She's smarter than me.
* I can't do anything right.
* I'm ugly.
* I never have anything to say.

4. How moody are you?

Ecstatic one minute and ready to bawl the next? Sure, everybody's got lots of different emotions, but are yours outta control? This quiz will reveal the truth.

DIRECTIONS: Check all the statements that sound like you.

- [ ] You have a reputation as a yeller.
- [ ] Everybody knows when you're PMSing.
- [ ] Some days you can barely get out of bed in the morning.
- [ ] Your moods are like a roller coaster—flying high, then dropping low.
- [ ] You often go to the nurse's office if you just aren't in the mood for class.
- [ ] Sometimes you're the life of the party, and other times you're a total wallflower.
- [ ] You frequently get into fights with your friends.
- [ ] There are times when you've wanted to talk to a counselor about your problems.
- [ ] When someone asks, "What's wrong?" you usually don't have an answer.
- [ ] Sometimes you just aren't in the mood to deal with certain friends.
- [ ] You think you might be depressed more often than the average person.
- [ ] You rarely hold back your really intense emotions or feelings.

- When something's wrong, you prefer to deal with it right away instead of waiting to think it over.
- Sometimes you make up excuses to get off the phone when you don't feel like talking.
- You have a bunch of different looks that you wear, depending on how you feel.

SCORING

Now count up the number of statements you checked and read the scoring section for your total below.

IF YOU CHECKED FOUR OR FEWER STATEMENTS: **Rock Steady**
How'd you get so cool? You're the master of your own emotions—you'd never cry in class, and you rarely feel like you want to crawl under a rock and hide out of embarrassment. Sure, there are some days when the blues strike or times when you're suddenly elated for no reason at all, but they definitely don't rule your life! You always act appropriately in public, and your friends know where they stand with you. If you don't see this steadiness in everyone around you, don't be surprised. Being this amazingly stable is a rare—and cool—trait!

IF YOU CHECKED FIVE TO NINE STATEMENTS: **Sorta Stable**
Okay, so you've been known to get a little weepy at Hallmark commercials. And sometimes when you're in a hideous mood, you'll snap at a friend. But you aren't completely ruled by your emotions, and in those rare cases where you freak out for no reason, you do damage control

ASAP and apologize. This level of moodiness is pretty normal—especially thanks to PMS and those insane teenage hormones. One tip: When you sense an evil mood creeping up on you, take cover. Spare your friends and family the wrath and veg in your room until you feel human again.

IF YOU CHECKED TEN OR MORE STATEMENTS: **Moody Mama**
Looks like you learned how to live life by watching soap operas. One minute you're in ecstasy, the next you're weeping mascara all over that pretty face of yours. And although it must be pretty exciting in your head, your friends and family are probably ready to pull their hair out from all the frustration! By flip-flopping between emotional highs and lows, you're going to drive away the people who care about you, since they never know if you're about to hug them or scream at them. To take a step toward stability, ask a friend or family member you trust to help you figure out your moods. Are there certain things (stress, body image woes) that always trigger your unhappiness? If you learn to cope with what's really bugging you, you'll become a lot more stable.

A Song for Every Mood!

If you're feelin' . . .	Listen to . . .
Dissed by a boy	"I Will Survive," by Gloria Gaynor
Ready to party	"Celebration," by Kool & the Gang
Ready to nap	"Stand by Me," by Ben E. King
Friendless	"Express Yourself," by Madonna
Gaga in love	"Summer Nights," from *Grease*, by John Travolta and Olivia Newton-John

5. How responsible are you?

When the teacher leaves the classroom, does she leave you in charge—or warn you that you'd better behave? Find out how dependable you are with this quiz.

1. Saturday you have an all-day baby-sitting gig—eight hours, three kids, one stressed-out you. How do you prepare for the challenge?

(a) You pack a bag of craft stuff, like yarn and construction paper, check out a few Web sites for fun activities to do with kids, and come up with a daylong schedule of fun.

(b) You bring along your address book so you can call up your buddies during your boring day.

(c) You wear comfy clothes so you can get down 'n' dirty playing all the games you loved as a kid, like hide-and-seek, Marco Polo, and Mother, may I.

2. Whoo-hoo! Your best friend passed her driver's test. She shows up at your door with her shiny new license and her mom's station wagon. How do you celebrate her driving achievement?

(a) Have your mom join you for a drive around the neighborhood. You'll drive alone with your friend once she has more experience.

(b) Tell your mom you're going out and that you don't know when you'll be back. This is your ticket to freedom.

(c) Have your friend drive you to Dairy Queen—on back roads—for a congratulations Blizzard.

3. A nasty flu has rendered you bathroom-bound for twenty-four hours, which means you can't even think about going to school. (Awww!) Which of these scenarios sounds like your top priority?

(a) Have your best friend drop off the homework assignments and make her stick around to give you the day's gossip.

(b) Call a person from each of your classes to get the homework and ask to copy their notes tomorrow.

(c) Turn on the TV and catch up on Jenny, Ricki, Jerry, and Montel. You'll get the assignments tomorrow.

4. You convince your parents that you're old enough to stay at home for the weekend by yourself while they go to your grandma's quilt-a-thon. When they come through the front door on Sunday night, what will they most likely notice first?

(a) The stereo system (the bass is thumping loud enough to rattle their teeth) and your group of friends hanging in the messy living room.

(b) The house is just like they left it, except for the pizza box by the garbage and a few soda cans on the coffee table.

(c) The house is totally gleaming—you spent the entire time cleaning and reorganizing the place.

5. Cha-ching! It's payday at The Slushie Station. When the check hits your hand, you sprint to the bank and

(a) get $20 cash for yourself, then deposit the rest.

(b) cash the whole thing—it's your play money for the week.

(c) deposit it in your savings account; textbooks and tuition will be way expensive someday.

Add up your points using the following answer key, then read the paragraph next to your total.

1. (a) 3, (b) 1, (c) 2
2. (a) 3, (b) 1, (c) 2
3. (a) 2, (b) 3, (c) 1
4. (a) 1, (b) 2, (c) 3
5. (a) 2, (b) 1, (c) 3

IF YOU SCORED 5 TO 7: **Duty Dodger**
You see commitments as massive roadblocks to fun—things to be avoided at all costs. Even if your gut says, "You really shouldn't," you make your decisions based on what makes you happy—instead of considering other people's feelings. The bonus? You're probably one pretty carefree girl. The bummer? You don't know what it feels like to be counted on and respected. You can still do damage control and rehab that rep. Start small, like by being more responsible with your money or by doing house chores as soon as your mom asks. Soon all those big responsibilities won't seem so scary anymore.

IF YOU SCORED 8 TO 12: **Completely Committed**
You've discovered a pretty sweet secret: Victory feels more amazing when you've worked hard to achieve it. For example, you'd be more proud of an A-plus if you studied hard for it instead of copying your neighbor's test paper. Before you accept a responsibility, whether it's watching a neighbor's cat or bringing cookies for a bake sale, you make sure you have the time and interest needed to do a good job—or you'll try to get out of it. Haven't found a graceful way

of saying no to people who need your help? Try honesty, as in, "I would love to help you out, but right now I don't have the time it would require to do a good job."

IF YOU SCORED 13 TO 15: **Obligation Obsessed**

You love it when people trust and respect you, and you often find yourself doing over-the-top prep work. Ultra-responsible girls like you always meet or exceed people's expectations, so you've developed a reputation as someone who can be counted on. But are you doing all this stuff because you want to—or because you want to impress people? If you find yourself stressed to the max with all your responsibilities, it's okay to say no. Commit to things you really enjoy—a team, a job, whatever—and steer clear of the rest. Responsibility should feel good, not like an energy vampire.

How to Get Your Parents to Trust You

✳ *Make Your Friends Mom-Friendly*

  Example: "I'm going to the movies with Maria, the straight-A student."

  Brag in front of your family about your friends' great grades, winning goals, or other achievements. It puts your worried parents at ease if they know you're out with someone who's proved she's responsible.

✳ *Play by Their Rules*

  Example: "I'll be in before curfew."

  Nothing freaks parents out more than when they catch you trying to pull a fast one on them. Follow their rules, no matter how unfair they seem. That will show them you're responsible, which'll result in fewer rules in the future.

❋ *Let Them See Your Scene*

Example: "We hung out at the food court for an hour, then went to the drugstore and tried on makeup samples, then Stacey's mom picked us up."

Instead of being mysterious and not telling your parents what you do when you're out, give them some idea of what you were up to. Otherwise they assume the worst and picture you playing darts in a smoke-filled bar while you claim to be "just hanging out."

6. Can you stand up for yourself?

When someone pushes you too hard, do you feel okay saying no? To discover whether you need to strengthen your tough-girl side, read on. . . .

1. You're in line at the CD store when a man shamelessly cuts right in front of you. How do you handle it?
> *(a) Think, "Hey! Jerk!" but give him a sweet little smile.*
> *(b) Say loudly, "Hey, mister, the back of the line is way back there," and point him in the right direction.*
> *(c) Tap him on the shoulder and say nicely, "Excuse me, but did you know that there's a line here?"*

2. You're at the salon, and the nice hairdresser is going to work on your 'do. The problem? She must have spaced when you told her, "Just a trim, please," 'cause she's turning your bob into a pixie cut. When she reaches for the electric trimmer, what do you do?

> (a) Repeat your instructions and mention that you're getting concerned that your hair's too short.
> (b) Buy a hat on the way home.
> (c) Yell, "Whoa! Are you crazy!" and demand to speak to the manager.

3. Sure, you love your best friend to death, but you notice that when you lend her money, she never, ever pays you back. When she asks to borrow two dollars for a snack after school, what do you do?

> (a) Hand over the cash. It's only two dollars, after all.
> (b) Give it to her but say, "This is the last time until I get paid back."
> (c) Tell her that she's cut off until you get all the cash back that she's borrowed.

4. As you're heading out the front door to meet your crush at the mall, your high-maintenance friend calls with a "crisis." How do you cope?

> (a) Tell her you're on your way out and offer to call her back tomorrow.
> (b) Invite her along to the mall, even though you know your guy was hoping it'd be just the two of you.
> (c) Ask her what's wrong, then after a few minutes tell her you'll stop by later that night.

5. Yeah, your boyfriend is cute. And sweet. And those dimples are to die for. But he's majorly flaky when it comes to being on time. In fact, he's supposed to pick you up for a date tonight at eight, but he doesn't show until nine. What do you do?

(a) Tell him you'd appreciate him calling when he's going to be late next time and give him one more chance to make it up to you.

(b) Hardly notice. After ten minutes of waiting, you called up other friends and went out for the night.

(c) Keep your mouth shut—you don't want to look picky and clingy.

SCORING

Add up your points, then read your scoring section below.

1. (a) 0, (b) 10, (c) 5
2. (a) 5, (b) 0, (c) 10
3. (a) 0, (b) 5, (c) 10
4. (a) 10, (b) 0, (c) 5
5. (a) 5, (b) 10, (c) 0

IF YOU SCORED 0 TO 15: **Pushover**

Yikes! You're like a human doormat. C'mon—you must've noticed it before. When you're faced with a situation that requires you to stand up for yourself, you back down. And that leaves you feeling pretty bummed. Sure, it's easier to go along with the crowd, but when you do that all the time, people stop respecting you—and more important, you stop respecting yourself. Go back through the quiz and read the five-point answers; then try to model your behavior after them from now on. You'll feel much better about yourself.

IF YOU SCORED 20 TO 30: **Perfectly Protected**

Hel-lo, little confident one! Although you wish you could avoid all those icky, confrontational situations in life, you know you can't—and that you need to protect yourself at times. It looks like you've mastered the balance of saying a laid-back "no" instead of an over-the-top "NO!!!" You're also great at helping friends if they're in trouble, but they know where you stand, so they won't try to walk all over you.

IF YOU SCORED 35 TO 50: **Pit Bull**

Nobody would ever accuse you of lacking a backbone. While it's great that you stand up for yourself, you have to learn to tame your anger and aggressiveness before people stop asking you for help altogether. If you keep up this scary attitude, you're gonna develop a reputation of being a big ole meanie. Learn to keep your temper and sarcasm under control, and you'll reap the true rewards of being self-reliant.

7. Could you be psychic?

Do you trust your cosmic instincts, or can you get by in life on facts alone?

1. You often wake up right before your alarm goes off. *True/False*

2. You get that spooky déjà vu feeling all the time. *True/False*

3. You think horoscopes are pretty on target. *True/False*

4. You can guess who's calling before you pick up the phone. *True/False*

5. You often finish your friends' or siblings' sentences. *True/False*

6. You go by your first impressions of people instead of waiting to get to know them. *True/False*

7. You frequently think about a friend you haven't talked to in a long time, then receive a letter or get a call from her soon after. *True/False*

8. Sometimes when you call a friend and get a busy signal, you find out later that she was trying to call you at that same moment. *True/False*

9. You think the fortunes in fortune cookies often come true. *True/False*

SCORING

Count up the number of times you selected true then find your answer section below.

IF YOU MARKED SIX TO NINE TRUES: **So Psychic, It's Spooky**

You could start your own 1-900 line! Seriously, you're very in touch with your intuitive side, which means you can easily pick up on other people's emotions and thoughts. Just be sure that you don't jump to conclusions about someone based purely on gut instinct; it could make you lose out on some potential pals.

IF YOU MARKED THREE TO FIVE TRUES: **Kinda Cosmically Connected**

Okay, so you aren't exactly a human Magic 8 Ball, but there are times when you just know stuff that there's no logica explanation for. Maybe you feel an ESP-type connection with certain family members or friends, and you can sense when they're in trouble. Trust your hunches, especially when it comes to these people—they're usually on target.

Astrologically Absent

Ah, you're so skeptical that you've actually talked yourself out of any psychic powers you might possess. You write off a lot of ESP-type moments as pure coincidence when really there might be more behind them. But think about it: Have there been times when your gut has told you to do something, and it ends up being the right thing? Sure, you might not want to bet your life's savings on the lottery, but it doesn't hurt to listen to that little voice in your head sometimes.

4

all about the
outer you

you've heard it a million times on those cheesy after-school specials: It's what's on the inside that counts. And while that's totally true, we bet that even the people who star in those TV shows brush their hair in the A.M. and bum out when they get zits. It's pretty normal to want to look good—after all, the outer you is the first impression most people get. The quizzes in this chapter will clue you in to what kind of signals your surface sends—and tell you how to change them if you don't dig what they're saying.

1. What's your perfect look?

What style of clothes, hair, and makeup go with the inner you? Take this quiz to find out!

1. While hanging in your bedroom, you smell smoke. Aack—there's a fire! Assuming that your family and all the pets have made it safely outside, what one personal item would you grab before rushing to safety?

(a) Your team jersey.

(b) Your journal.

(c) Your photo album.

(d) Your CD collection.

2. Which of these creatures would you dress up as for Halloween?

(a) An alien, wearing head-to-toe silver and tinting your hair purple for the evening.

(b) A ghost, cutting two eyeholes in an old sheet and making full-on spooky sounds.

(c) A football player, with full padding, a helmet, and a blacked-out tooth.

(d) An angel, with real feather wings and a sparkly halo.

3. You can't help going out of control when you shop at

(a) vintage clothes stores.

(b) a sporting goods store.

(c) out-of-the-way stores in the city that have really original stuff.

(d) the mall, where they have everything in your size and a variety of colors.

4. When it comes to the subject of your hair, people would most likely say

(a) it always looks nice, with every strand in place, and she's had the same style for a while.

(b) you never know what she's gonna do next; she isn't afraid of a dramatic cut.

(c) she loves fancy updos and flowery hair accessories.

(d) it's usually pulled back, like in a ponytail.

5. Luck is totally on your side! You win a magazine contest, which means they'll come and redecorate your room with one of the following styles. Which would you pick?

(a) The game-room theme, with a Ping-Pong table and beanbag chairs to sit in while you play every video game on the planet (on a big-screen TV!).

(b) The futuristic room, with an awesome sound system, inflatable furniture, mood lighting, and a rotating closet.

(c) The organizational makeover—as in, you really like your room the way it is, but you'd be psyched for them to come in and reorganize everything.

(d) The fantasy room, with a canopy bed, fluffy carpets, an insane stuffed animal collection, and an amazing vanity area for you to apply makeup.

6. If you wanted to make your essay on "What I Want to Be When I Grow Up" really stand out from the pile on your teacher's desk, what would you do?

(a) Use pretty paper and write the title in your fanciest handwriting.

(b) Create a fancy cover page on the computer and print it out in color.

(c) Do your essay up to look like a magazine, with cutout pictures inside.

(d) Make a collage report cover out of pictures from the sports pages.

7. You almost always go for guys who
   (a) get good grades or are popular.
   (b) are on a team.
   (c) could get away with wearing nail polish or hair highlights.
   (d) are into writing or playing an instrument.

8. Your ultimate Saturday night would involve
   (a) going to a dance club and meeting a cute guy.
   (b) having a moonlight picnic with the guy you like.
   (c) getting together with a group of friends and having a party.
   (d) dinner and a movie with your crush.

SCORING

In the grid below, circle the letter you chose for each question.

1.	a	d	c	b
2.	c	a	b	d
3.	b	c	d	a
4.	d	b	a	c
	S	**F**	**C**	**R**

5.	a	b	c	d
6.	d	c	b	a
7.	b	c	a	d
8.	c	a	d	b
	S	**F**	**C**	**R**

Now find the vertical column with the most circles. See that letter at the bottom of the column? Read the answer section for that letter below.

S Is for SPORTY

You're always on the go, so you need a look that can keep up with your active lifestyle.

What to get: A few pairs of ultracool sneakers in bright, funky colors that you'll wear off the field. Some track pants with side stripes and ankle zippers. A cool hooded windbreaker. Fitted T-shirts in bright colors to replace those baggy white ones.

What to get rid of: Aside from saying bye-bye to baggy white tees, quit wearing your field sneakers at non-sporting events. Also, bag the worn-out sweatpants and sweatshirts—they give off a big-time I-don't-care-what-I-look-like vibe.

Why don'tcha try: Okay, so you aren't into much makeup. That's cool. But a sporty girl like you can get away with this supersimple look: Brush on a bronzing powder—it should be applied to the places where the sun naturally highlights your face (forehead, nose, cheekbones, chin). Then dab on some lip gloss for a cool shine. For a sweet nighttime look, add a coat of mascara.

F Is for FUNKY

Dressing like everybody else would drive you nuts. You're completely original, and you need a look that makes you stand apart from the rest.

What to get: A subscription to a fashion mag like *Vogue*. A pair of leather jeans is a funky basic that'll last forever. Cool eyeglasses with thick frames—whether they're prescription or not. Lots of hair accessories like headbands, clips, and bobby pins—you need 'em to keep up with your cutting-edge styles.

What to get rid of: Ultratrendy items you bought more than a year ago and haven't worn in the last six months; a clotheshorse like you needs all the closet space she can get. Also, give away shoes that are really painfully uncomfortable (your feet will thank you). Trash anything that's permanently stained—give it an honorable discharge from your wardrobe.

Why don'tcha try: Temporary hair color in an out-there shade, like blue or pink. Even coloring a few strands will look neat. Also, take old nail polishes and mix them up to create an original shade. You can find some cool treasures at vintage stores—and you're practically guaranteed to be the only one at school wearing 'em!

C Is for CLASSIC

You have a timeless style—and probably a reputation for always looking flawless.

What to get: Low-heeled, knee-high boots look cool yet classic with skirts. When you find a shirt that fits perfectly, why not buy two? Don't forget to incorporate red and sky blue in your closet full of white, black, and gray—they're classic colors that keep you from looking too monochromatic.

What to get rid of: Clothes that don't fit, even if you love them. (Give 'em away to charity.) Whether it's a pair of shoes or your favorite belt, anything that you've worn for the past three years probably looks sort of grungy by now. Don't get sentimental; get rid of it instead.

Why don'tcha try: Go a little wild with your hair. Instead of pulling it back in a plain ponytail, make a far-side part and sleek it back in a low tail instead. And remember: Classy, classic chicas like you usually look outstanding in red lipstick.

R Is for ROMANTIC

You're right in the middle of your own real-life fairy tale. You like daydreaming, and you believe in love at first sight.

What to get: Long skirts, which are back in a big way. Also, peasant blouses with drawstring-neck details. Anything with a light floral pattern (but only one piece at a time, thankyouverymuch). An adorable, floppy fishing hat can even make jeans and a tee a cute, girlie outfit.

What to get rid of: White panty hose, anything lacy, anything with more ruffles than a prom dress. Be sure to repair vintage clothes—they look cool when they're in good shape, but otherwise they can look just plain old.

Why don'tcha try: Sewing some freehand embroidery on an old pair of jeans—a few daisies would look cute. Also, when you think of romantic tresses, you think curly, right?

So let your natural waves free (apply mousse to wet hair and let air-dry). Got straight hair? Put a bunch of loose braids in wet hair, then go to sleep. In the A.M. you'll have slinky waves.

2. How does your body image rate?

Does the image in your mirror have a huge impact on your moods and thoughts? Answer these questions to see whether you're giving too much thought to your looks and weight.

DIRECTIONS: Grade each statement with a **1** (if it's something you never do or think), **2** (if it's something you sometimes do or think), or **3** (if it's something you do or think all the time).

1. When I look in the mirror, I like what I see.

2. I exercise to stay healthy, not to look like Ally McBeal.

3. I wear clothes that accentuate my figure.

4. I don't mind clothes shopping.

5. If a guy was staring at me as I walked down the hall, I'd think it's because I look good.

6. I never call myself fat.

7. When I see myself in pictures, I usually think I look good.

8. I have good posture.

9. When I walk, I keep my head up.

10. When I talk about my body, I don't use phrases

that start with, "Someday I'll . . ." (as in, "lose weight," "get taller," etc.)

■ **11.** I try to eat well but don't freak out about indulging in goodies once in a while.

■ **12.** I have a swimsuit that I'm not embarrassed to wear.

■ **13.** I don't mind going out in casual clothes, without makeup on.

■ **14.** When I grow out of clothes, I get rid of them instead of keeping them in my closet.

■ **15.** I don't dream of getting plastic surgery someday.

SCORING

Add up the numbers you wrote in the blanks, then read your answer section below.

IF YOU SCORED 15 TO 25: **Body Bummed**
Ouch! You are your own worst critic, friend. Why do you beat yourself up like this? You need some body image rehab stat! Start being as supportive of yourself as you are of your best friend. For example, you'd never in a million years say, "Ugh, you're so fat," to her, would you? Make a conscious effort to treat yourself like your best friend—and let no more negativity cross those luscious lips of yours.

IF YOU SCORED 26 TO 35: **Body Balanced**
Psst! Here's a secret: While you're sitting there, wondering why that guy's staring at you, he's self-consciously wondering why you're staring at him. And that's the thing

about body image—most people have some insecurities, like you. But if you can work through them (and get over them), you'll be much happier. How? Penalize yourself for every negative thought you have. The payment: Say three nice things about yourself after a criticism slips out. Soon body bliss will come naturally to you.

IF YOU SCORED 36 TO 45: **Body Blissed**
Amazing! You're in on a little secret: If you walk with confidence, people will see you in a much more positive light. Think about it—you spy someone with hunched shoulders, shyly staring at her shoes. What do you think about her? That she's self-conscious, which hardly makes you eager to meet her. But your body lingo says you know you're all that—you practically ooze confidence from your pores! It turns you into a people magnet, with everyone wondering what your secret is. Keep it up!

Secrets of the Stars

❋ Before you set your sights on looking just like the models you see in magazines, listen up: Don't be fooled by photos! The celebs aren't as perfect as they look. Certain computer programs exist for the sole purpose of erasing zits, smoothing out tummy bulges, filling in weird tooth gaps, lightening under-eye circles. . . . Get the idea? As far as on-screen beauty goes, actors and actresses have literally a team of experts working on them—from makeup artists to hairstylists to wardrobe specialists. In fact, if you were to see your fave celebs walking down the street, you might not recognize them because they look (gasp!) human. So don't compare yourself to celebrities 'cause the truth is, even they don't naturally look as good as you think!

3. What's your color personality?

From the "who knew" files: There's a hue to match every personality type in the world. So are you rebel red or sympathetic blue? Answer these questions and find out.

DIRECTIONS: Check all the statements that sound like you

- I have a talent for making things grow.
- I have a major soft spot for animals.
- I spend lots of time outside.
- I come up with many great ideas but only follow through with a few.
- I usually keep my feelings to myself.
- People tease me for being such a girlie-girl.
- If I had to pick, I'd prefer living in the country over living in the city.
- I can always motivate my friends to go out.
- My friends can count on me, even if it means I have to break a rule for them.
- Sometimes I cancel plans if I don't feel like going out.
- I love to read or draw.
- When I promise a friend something, I don't give up until I deliver.

🌳   Recycling is important to me.

⚡   I've gone to the movies or a restaurant by myself.

✦   I go out of my way to make others happy but rarely do it to please myself.

♥   If I really need money, I ask my parents for it.

☁   I always remember what people wore to a party, even if I didn't consciously take note.

✦   I love hanging out in big groups of people.

👄   I'm not afraid of anything.

☁   I've had lots of the same friends for several years.

✦   My clothes have to be comfortable, or I'll go crazy.

🔥   I'm always the one who starts the marathon joke-telling sessions with my friends.

🌳   I have a few things that I collect.

👄   I jump at the chance to try new things— the riskier they are, the better.

⚡   I have a talent for reading people's thoughts.

🔥   If I sit still for too long, I get bored.

👄   People often say that I become obsessed with my crushes.

♥   I tend to be shy around new people.

✦   Things always seem to work out for me, so I don't worry much.

👄	▨	I'm the head of several school clubs or activities.
⚡	▨	People often think I'm older than I really am.
🌿	▨	Taking risks is something I love to do.
✦	▨	I'm very optimistic, and if I think my loved ones are bummin' over something silly, I'll tell them.
⚡	▨	I'm a good listener, but I don't get too wrapped up in others' problems.
🌿	▨	Every school year I pick out a few new friends.

SCORING

Count up the number of times you selected each shape and read the answer section next to the shape you selected most.

Number of 🌳 s: ___
Number of ♥ s: ___
Number of ☁ s: ___
Number of ✦ s: ___
Number of 👄 s: ___
Number of ⚡ s: ___
Number of 🌿 s: ___

IF YOU CHOSE MOSTLY 🌳 s: **Green Goddess**
You're at your best when you're outside—it's like you soak up energy from all the living things around you! Also, friends know that you're incredibly trustworthy. In fact, you love taking care of them. But . . . change isn't one of your most fave things on the planet; that means you can get a little

stubborn. In fact, sometimes you can be downright greedy with your possessions. Don't forget to share, greenie.

IF YOU CHOSE MOSTLY ♥ S: **Tickled Pink**

Hug much? Thought so. Pink girls like you are very loving and physically affectionate. It tears you up inside to fight with your friends and family. You'd much rather overlook their little flaws and live a peaceful life. But . . . you can be very hard to get to know—and people may misread that as being snobby. Also, you don't like to make waves, which means you're a little squeamish about stating your opinions. Share the love, pinky.

IF YOU CHOSE MOSTLY ☁ S: **True Blue**

Nah—this isn't like boo-hoo blue. It's more like cool blue—the truly devoted friend. You're a quick learner—knowledge practically clings to your brain, and you're extra sharp when it comes to science and art. But . . . your loyalty sometimes gets you taken advantage of because you're so blindly faithful that you won't walk away from a friendship—even if you're the one doing all the work.

IF YOU CHOSE MOSTLY ✦ S: **Not-Too-Mellow Yellow**

You tend to look on the bright side of things, and you're always the most easygoing, cheerful face in the crowd. People get a sense of power when they're around you—it's almost like your happiness is contagious. But . . . even though go-with-the-flow golden girls like you sometimes go out of their way to please other people, they also can be a little lazy when nobody's looking. Don't forget to treat yourself as well as you treat others, sunshine.

IF YOU CHOSE MOSTLY 👄 s: **Fiery Red**
You're such a firecracker! When you decide to go for something, you do it with 100 percent effort and you won't give up until you get the job done. Bravery comes pretty naturally to you; in fact, not much freaks you out. But . . . in your quest to be the best, some red girls tend to bulldoze over their quieter friends. Use your powerful personality for good, and stop giving in to your red-hot temper so much.

IF YOU CHOSE MOSTLY ⚡ s: **Deep Black**
You always get noticed, even though you don't care if you get attention. That's because you naturally ooze charm and sophistication. Black personalities love their solo time and are huge fans of quietly observing others. But . . . you tend to be a little shy, and people can mistake that for being secretive or antisocial. Let people in on the fact that you're naturally pretty curious.

IF YOU CHOSE MOSTLY 🍃 s: **Orange You Happy?**
Most of the time you're on the go—and that's what keeps you energetic 24/7. Vegging in front of the TV kind of turns you off. You'd rather be in action, hanging out with your friends and doing all sorts of cool activities. But . . . your constant quest for a good time means you can get into serious trouble. Remember not to go overboard on your way to having a good time.

4. Which workout works best for you?

Are you most motivated when part of a team? Or do you groove on challenging yourself? Find out the sports that suit you best with these Q's.

1. When others are depending on you, you usually
   (a) do better because you hate letting people down.
   (b) do just as well as you would by yourself.
   (c) do worse than you normally would because you're stressed out by the extra pressure.

2. Which of the following is closest to your top reason for working out?
   (a) It's fun.
   (b) I like to stay in shape, and I enjoy playing sports.
   (c) I like to push myself and see how far I can go.

3. In order for you to get better at something, you need to
   (a) watch others and learn their tricks.
   (b) practice.
   (c) concentrate on your form and focus.

4. You tend to go for sports that
   (a) give you a chance to work on the same team as others.
   (b) give you a chance to play against one opponent.
   (c) you can do completely alone.

5. To you, winning is

    (a) getting more points or goals than the other team.

    (b) not letting the other person score.

    (c) doing better than you did last time.

SCORING

Count up the number of times you selected each letter and read the answer section next to the letter you selected most.

IF YOU CHOSE MOSTLY A'S: **Go, Team!**

You do best when people are counting on you. Plus in order for you to stick with a sport or workout, it's gotta be not only social but fun!

Sports That Suit You:

* ✻ Teamwork-focused stuff like volleyball, soccer, field hockey, softball, basketball.
* ✻ In-line skating with friends.
* ✻ Aerobics classes.

IF YOU CHOSE MOSTLY B'S: **Challenge-Me Champion**

You like to focus on one opponent rather than an entire team. It gives you the chance to perfect your skills as you face each new challenger's set of talents.

Sports That Suit You:

* ✻ One-on-one activities like tennis, track, fencing.
* ✻ Frisbee, bowling, or Ping-Pong.
* ✻ Kick-boxing classes.

5. What's your body type?

Are you a Vata, Pitta, or Kapha? No, they aren't sorority names; they're body types. And a five-thousand-year-old Indian system of medicine says that the shape you fall into determines the best foods and exercises for you. Read on to find your figure!

DIRECTIONS: Check all the statements that sound like you.

1. You could sleep through marching band practice.
2. People often say you're a good leader.
3. After a fight, you forgive and forget.
4. People always come to you for a shoulder to cry on.
5. During sad movies you always cry.
6. Some foods totally upset your stomach.

7. Hunger always strikes you at the same time every day.
8. Your bedroom has looked mostly the same for the past three years.
9. You never forget if someone hurts you.
10. You always get amazing grades.
11. Even you have to admit that you worry too much.
12. You often wake up in the middle of the night.
13. You can develop big, strong muscles quickly.
14. You freeze up when you have a tight deadline.
15. You hate making big decisions.
16. You can still find some items to fit you in the kids' clothing department.
17. You're very competitive.
18. People have trouble keeping up with your normal walking pace.
19. Guys often pick you to be on their team in gym.
20. You hate sleeping in a stuffy room.
21. You quickly master new video games.
22. The best part of waking up is having breakfast.
23. You change your crushes often.
24. Hot weather drains your energy.
25. Having a packed schedule freaks you out.
26. When you get a good grade, you reward yourself with a yummy treat.
27. You always follow through with your promises.

In the grid below, circle the numbers of all the statements you checked. Find the column in which you have the most circles. Read the answer section for that letter below.

A	B	C
1	3	2
4	6	7
5	11	10
8	12	14
9	16	17
13	18	19
15	21	20
22	23	24
26	25	27

IF YOU SELECTED MOSTLY A'S: **Kapha Queen**

Inner Kapha qualities: You understand people well—many talk show hosts, like Oprah, Ricki, and Jenny Jones, have this body type. You're slow, steady, and totally dependable, and it takes a whole lot to get you angry.

Outer Kapha qualities: You probably have a slow metabolism, which means you put on weight easily. Out-of-balance Kaphas may have sinus problems or feel tired frequently.

Cool foods for Kaphas: Half of every day's menu should be fruits and vegetables, and you should try to make room for at least one salad a day.

Get-moving tips: Kaphas are into chilling out, which means that exercise isn't usually on your top ten list. But with your strength and dedication, you have what it takes to be a great swimmer, runner, or bicyclist.

IF YOU SELECTED MOSTLY B'S: **Little Miss Vata**

Inner Vata qualities: Vatas like you are usually totally talkative and quick thinkers. You make friends easily, and you're a big worrier. Warning—when you get upset, you blow up with almost no warning.

Outer Vata qualities: Vatas are usually thin and always on the move. You're also very flexible. You get cold easily and sometimes get cramps.

Cool foods for Vatas: With a delicate stomach like yours, it's recommended that you eat warm, comforting foods—rice, potatoes—instead of raw stuff.

Get-moving tips: Vatas thrive at relaxing or disciplined sports, like yoga, golf, ballet, and gymnastics.

IF YOU SELECTED MOSTLY C'S: **Pitta Sister**

Inner Pitta qualities: You aren't afraid to speak your mind—and you're really good at putting your thoughts into words. Passionate girls like you always blow people away. But you can also be a little too critical and competitive.

Outer Pitta qualities: You have a naturally athletic build, and you're fairly strong. Sometimes you get hot flashes.

Cool foods for Pittas: Your appetite can get out of control quickly, so when you feel hunger pangs, you'd better act quickly. If you don't, you'll be tired and grumpy. Steer clear of spicy foods, which ignite your already hot nature. *Get-moving tips:* Since you're so fiery naturally, the exercises you choose should be mellowing, as in hiking, diving, and snowboarding.

6. Do you eat right?

Okay, so you know that, like, eating Doritos at every meal isn't a good idea. But do you know the facts about nutrition? You should, 'cause eating right affects everything, from your looks to your brainpower. Test your nutrition know-how with this quiz, then pick up some helpful tips on how to eat healthier.

1. Skipping meals helps you lose weight. *True/False*

2. If you can, you should eliminate all fat from your diet. *True/False*

3. You don't really need to eat at least five servings of fruits and veggies a day. *True/False*

4. Fat-free means "all you can eat." *True/False*

5. You should never eat snacks or desserts. *True/False*

6. Drinking juice is just as good for you as eating a piece of fruit. *True/False*

7. If you eat a really big dinner one night, you should work out twice as hard the next day. *True/False*

8. It doesn't matter how fast you eat. *True/False*

SCORING

Check out the answer key below to see how many questions you got right. Then make sure you read all the explanations to learn how to be an expert on healthy eating!

1. False

While skipping meals may make the number on the scale go down for a day, the weight loss is temporary. You'll probably notice it's back in a day or two. The only healthy weight-loss method is a well-balanced diet and regular exercise!

2. False

Wrong! Fat is a nutrient, and it's just as important to your body as proteins and carbs. For a good-for-you diet, most nutritionists say that no more than 30 percent of your calories a day should come from fat.

3. False

We know—this one's a toughie. But you should eat five to nine (!) servings of fruits and veggies a day in order to make sure you're getting enough of all the important vitamins and nutrients.

4. False

Eating fat-free or low-fat foods is usually better than chowing on their full-fat counterparts, but there is a limit to how much you should eat. These foods still contain sugar, salt, and calories! Pay attention to the serving size on the back of packages.

5. False

In moderation, eating desserts isn't bad for you—it's

when you skip the meal and head straight to the cake that's the problem. In fact, if you deprive yourself of what you really want, you may continue eating to fill the void.

6. False
Both are good for you, but chewing up the actual fruit is best for your body.

7. False
Nope—it's all about balance, friend. You shouldn't overexercise to punish yourself for overeating. Just learn to say no earlier next time—like, before the third helping.

8. False
It takes your stomach about twenty minutes to feel full. So the slower you eat, the more time your body has to realize it doesn't need everything on your plate. Also, taking the time to chew your food thoroughly helps digestion.

5

all about
school

it's the place where you spend most of your waking hours— well, not counting that nap in study hall. So when you put together your favorite parts (lunch and, well, lunch) and your least-fave parts (who came up with chemistry, anyway?), do you get six hours of bliss or boredom? The quizzes in this chapter will reveal your academic personality and shed light on the kinds of activities you might enjoy after class.

1. Do you study like a pro?

Could your study style be stressing you out? To discover how big your procrastination streak is, answer these questions.

1. Your English teacher assigns an eight-page essay, due in two weeks. Which of the following sounds most like your work schedule?

(a) You'll go to the library every day after school and work your butt off until it's done.

(b) You'll start in a few days and work hard, probably finishing the day before it's due.

(c) You'll start it a day or two before it's due and maybe pull an all-nighter. An ultratight deadline helps keep you focused.

2. First you wake up late. Then you mistake your hair spray bottle for deodorant. And now your math teacher springs a pop quiz on you. How do you deal?

(a) Stress out and obsess over how this will pull your grade down.

(b) Quickly flip through your notes to refresh your memory.

(c) Panic—you usually don't do your math homework, so you're in serious trouble. You ask to peek at your neighbor's notes.

3. Surprise! Class participation will count for extra credit in science tomorrow. To prepare, tonight you will

(a) reread the entire chapter and make flash cards, which you'll use to memorize every single fact.

(b) review the end-of-chapter questions and read your notes.
(c) wait until the teacher asks questions you know tomorrow, then put up your hand—or skip the extra credit altogether.

4. Which sounds most like your homework philosophy?
(a) You get to work soon after you get home, then continue after dinner, which means you have less than zero time for sports and clubs.
(b) An hour or two gets set aside every day, but you squeeze in some TV and social stuff.
(c) You don't usually do homework, or you do it quickly before bed or right before class.

5. You get a B on a midterm in your hardest class. The future rocket scientist who sits next to you got a B-minus. That means
(a) you still didn't study enough since you didn't get an A.
(b) your studying paid off—it's a hard class.
(c) there must be some freak grading mistake, or you just got very lucky.

6. Tick-tick-tick—the New Year's countdown is, um, counting down. So if you had to make a resolution about school, which would most likely come out of your mouth as the clock strikes twelve?
(a) I'm going to do whatever it takes to get the best grades in the whole class.
(b) I'm going to push myself to do better in the classes where I've been slacking.
(c) I'm going to start paying attention in class.

7. You hang up the phone and think, "Oh. My. God." Your crush-since-fourth-grade just invited you to the movies. But then there's the little matter of homework— your math teacher alone gave you enough to keep you busy until dawn. Once you do a little victory dance, you

(a) call him back and tell him you have to stay home. Maybe you can get together this weekend?

(b) ask for a rain check on the movie but see if he wants to meet you at the library for a study sesh.

(c) go to the movie and deal with the homework thing later . . . maybe.

SCORING

IF YOU SELECTED MOSTLY A'S: **Hooked on Pressure**
Notice symptoms like trouble sleeping, upset stomach, and serious moodiness? Ding! Ding! Ding! We have a class-A stress junkie! You're demanding top performance from yourself every day of your life—which is the yellow-brick road to getting burned out.

You get applause for your self-discipline and drive to succeed. Not a day goes by where you don't impress someone. Teachers know they can count on you to do your homework, and your parents' car bumper is covered with those My Kid Is an Honor Student stickers. It's almost like they expect you to earn A's, huh?

Here's one lesson you might not know: People respect you for you, not just for your grades. So the smart move may be to ease up the study pressure and apply that dedication to something that brings you big-time joy— sports, hanging out with friends, writing poetry. Get into the habit of telling your family what topics you're studying instead of what grades you're earning. With a little balance, you'll still be an awesome student—and you'll be a happier person, too.

IF YOU SELECTED MOSTLY B'S: **In the Study Zone**

You work hard, which earns you the right to play hard. The night before a nightmare-inducing test, you're certain to be studying instead of surfing the Web—and that's the path that'll lead you to school success. But you also know how to stay balanced, so you don't feel guilty relaxing with your friends and loafing in front of the TV every now and then.

You try hard because you want to be proud of yourself instead of striving to please your teacher or impress your classmates. That means you're very likely to succeed in college and beyond. Also, you have tons of brain confidence—so even if you get a C (eek!), you know you're not a dummy.

But there is a teensy-tiny risk for girls who study like you: Do you sometimes coast through undemanding classes, seeing them as a minivacation? Just because a subject comes easy to you doesn't mean you should cruise; think of it as an all-you-can-eat learning buffet instead.

IF YOU SELECTED MOSTLY C'S: **Secret Stress Case**

You're probably way open to learning, but you want it to be on your own terms—not stuck in a classroom or sitting at home behind a pile of books. Problem is, that's not the way school works.

So it's time to take a look at the way you're dealing (or not dealing) with studying. The fact is, you are stressed by school, but your stress comes from the embarrassment of being unprepared and worrying about failing. C'mon—admit it: When you hand your parents that report card, your heart pounds. And the reason for it is that Mom and Dad are in on your little secret: You could do a lot better if you tried.

But how do you start? In small ways. Try to eliminate a time waster from your schedule this week—whether it's writing notes to your friends in class or watching soap operas every day after school. And (here's the tricky part) use that time to focus on school. When you start to notice a difference, you'll feel proud (and less stressed) and ready to take the next step: eliminating another time waster.

The Lamest I-Don't-Have-My-Homework Excuses of All Time

* "I caught a virus from my computer and kept crashing all night."
* "I got grounded and wasn't allowed to leave my room. Unfortunately, my backpack was down in the living room."
* "The dog ate it."
* "The FBI confiscated it. A matter of national security. I can answer no further questions."
* "My horoscope said I would be taking a trip today, so I figured I wouldn't need to do it."
* "I got my braces off after school yesterday and didn't get home in time for schoolwork." (Hint: Don't use this one if you currently wear braces.)

2. Are you a joiner or a loner?

In order to find the best clubs and activities for you, you need to know if you enjoy depending on others or if you prefer being the captain of your own ship.

DIRECTIONS: Check off all the statements that sound like you.

1. On a rainy Saturday afternoon you'd rather read a book than play a board game with a friend.
2. You'd rather be on a student council committee than be a class officer.
3. You find it hard to concentrate when there's a lot of noise.
4. When a science project is assigned, you'd rather do it with a partner than fly solo.
5. Giving a speech in front of the entire class freaks you out so badly—you can't sleep the night before.
6. You're very comfortable asking friends for favors.
7. In your dream job you'd be really independent or maybe even self-employed.
8. You do your best when other people are depending on you.
9. Before you make a major decision, you think it over alone instead of going to friends for advice.
10. When you give advice, people usually follow it.

11. You aren't involved in many of the same activities as your closest friends.

12. When your parents set a rule that you think is unfair, you talk to them about it in a calm way.

13. You usually don't procrastinate.

14. You get your best studying done in groups.

15. Your team is doomed if you don't have a good coach.

16. Sometimes you enter a room and forget why you came in.

17. You're uncomfortable speaking up when you disagree with someone's opinion.

18. When teachers write comments on your essays, you're careful not to make that same mistake again.

19. You're most creative privately, at home.

20. You take criticism well.

SCORING

Count up the number of odd- and even-numbered statements that you selected and see which you have more of. Then read the scoring section that applies to you.

IF YOU SELECTED MOSTLY ODD-NUMBERED STATEMENTS:
Gimme-Serious-Solitude Girl

Flying solo totally energizes you. You love the idea of making quick decisions without the bother of getting a whole team organized. Another bonus: You're pretty unfazed by peer pressure; instead you keep a clear head and go for your own goals instead of worrying about what everybody else thinks.

What you need to work on is patience. When you're in group situations, you tend to get frustrated. If your team members in gym were goofing around instead of focusing on playing, you'd get annoyed—fast. And if the group you've been assigned for a class project isn't working quickly enough for you, you'll probably freak out. Working with others takes more time, but it can also have big rewards—friendship, new skills, more fun.

Below are some great get-involved ideas that should suit your independent streak and help you experiment with group activities.

✳ *Become a Writer for the Student Newspaper*

Bonuses: You'll love the independence of thinking up story ideas and finding people to interview. Plus you'll thrive under the pressure of meeting a deadline.

Your big challenge: This activity requires you to be part of a staff, which isn't something that puts stars in your eyes. For example, if you come up with a story idea and the editor says it stinks (Ouch!), you'll have to respect that and come up with a new idea—a struggle for a strong-willed girl like you.

✳ *Learn to Play an Instrument*

Bonuses: You have the extreme self-motivation needed for this activity. Putting in serious solo practice hours actually sounds appealing to you.

Your big challenge: If you decide to join the band, your frustration-o-meter may reach new highs when band practice goes at a slower pace than you'd like. Even if you've mastered a tune, other band members may need more time—and that could stretch your patience.

✳ *Do the Community-Service Thing*

Bonuses: By organizing a bake sale or campuswide cleanup day, you get the warm, fuzzy feeling of making the world (or your school) a better place. But your commitment is over in a day, so you won't have to deal with all the red tape of being involved in student government.

Your big challenge: You'll feel a little strange asking people for help. After all, if you worked for an entire weekend, you could probably make enough cookies for a one-woman bake sale. But that's not sharing the feel-good vibes that come from helping others. And besides, think of how many dishes you'd have to wash after that baking spree. . . .

IF YOU SELECTED MOSTLY EVEN-NUMBERED STATEMENTS:

Miss The-More-the-Merrier

You like to surround yourself with fun, creative people because that's how you get excited to go for goals. When you're alone, you're easily distracted by little stuff—the phone, the TV, the comfy bed calling for naptime. . . . But in a group you're very energized, and you're a great person to bounce around ideas with.

But there is a catch in being a joiner. Do you have a hard time focusing on things that need to be done when you're all alone? Without others to motivate you, you tend to procrastinate. Also, even if you're interested in a certain hobby or activity (riding horses, acting, writing poetry, um—skydiving), you won't pursue it unless you can find a friend to tag along with you.

So that means it may be time to stretch those wings of independence. Nope, that doesn't mean you should become a hermit; it's more like becoming comfortable doing what you want even if the crowd doesn't follow. Try out some of the activities listed below to play around with solo work while still getting all the benefits of being a group girl.

* *Take on a Leadership Role at School*

Bonuses: You'll get to soak up all the creative juices of people who want to get things done. Plus you'll be surrounded by those who are interested in hearing your opinion—which you're always more than happy to give!

Your big challenge: As a student government rep, you'll get to make rules. But will you be able to put your foot down when you have an opinion that's different from everybody else's? Your go-with-the-flow style will need some taming in order for you to be a great leader.

* *Be a Tutor or Start a Study Group*

Bonuses: Face it: You need motivation in order to kick into high study gear. And there's no better way for you to do homework than by turning it into a social thing. Helping younger kids or getting a study group together once a week are both great ways to boost your brainpower and have fun at the same time.

Your big challenge: Sure, it's easy to get a little distracted when you're surrounded by cool people—just make sure that you study school stuff (not your crush). Make it fun by quizzing one another with flash cards or turning an assignment into a game show.

❋ *Be a Peer Counselor*

Bonuses: You love it when people depend on you, and you're great at giving advice. So you can get involved by volunteering at a local teen hot line or go to the guidance counselor's office and volunteer to show new students around school.

Your big challenge: Social butterflies like you sometimes have a hard time keeping secrets. So if you were to be a peer counselor, you'd have to work to keep your lips sealed when people reveal their deepest secrets to you.

❋ *Take Up a Hobby of Your Own*

Bonuses: You'll be able to do it anytime, even when your friends are all busy. Try reading or skating or hey, even stamp collecting.

Your big challenge: You'll have to force yourself to get used to spending time alone. But you may actually find that you enjoy some solitude now and then.

3. What does your locker say about you?

That little metal box is like your home away from home. So by taking a peek inside, you can actually find out a lot about your inner self—priorities, likes, dislikes, astrological sign. (Okay, maybe not your sign. . . .)

DIRECTIONS: Check off all the items in the following list that sound like you, then discover their secret meaning in the next section.

☐ At end-of-year locker-clean-out time, I often find things I thought I'd lost. (1)

☐ I have a magnetic mirror on the door. (2)

☐ My friends all know my locker combo. (3)

☐ My locker is pretty empty because I usually stash my stuff in my friend's locker. (4)

☐ I cover the inside with magazine pics of cute boys. (5)

☐ I always keep a jacket in my locker in case I get cold. (6)

☐ There's sometimes a weird smell that comes from my locker—it's gym clothes or old food, I think. (7)

☐ I put cute or cool stickers all over the inside of my locker. (8)

SCORING

Find the number at the end of all the statements you checked. Then read the definition next to those numbers below to find out your locker personality.

(1): Pack-Rat Patty

You get emotionally attached to stuff pretty easily, which means you have a hard time letting go of things you really don't need—old tests, soda cans for recycling, science projects. . . .

What this means: You are a fiercely loyal friend, even when someone isn't being good to you anymore. Watch out for getting used by so-called friends who don't give back to you—in other words, do a little spring cleaning more often.

(2): Security-Seeking Sarah

Obviously you worry about your looks—but is there anybody who doesn't? If you just use this mirror to check for pepperoni in your teeth, that's cool. But if they're critical once-overs that leave you feeling bad about yourself, it may be time to take that mirror down.

What this means: For you, looking good gives you confidence—whether you use it to speak up in class or just to talk to your crush in the hall. But you are your own harshest critic. You may need to derive confidence from something inside you—your quick thinking, your great sense of humor. The image of you in the mirror isn't truly the real you.

(3): Nothing-to-Hide Nina

Your locker is an extension of you, so you can't imagine not giving your friends the key. They're welcome to your notebooks, munchie stash, or fave sweatshirt.

What this means: You're very generous and open with your friends. If you didn't want friends to see the real you, you'd probably be more secretive about your locker digits.

(4): Closeness-Lovin' Carrie

Sharing your friend's locker gives your day another social sunny spot. Plus the intimacy of sharing such a small space makes you feel close to your bud.

What this means: The idea of being alone may freak you out a little. You'd rather roam the halls with your friends than fly solo (which leaves you feelin' a little self-conscious). You also may be afraid of losing your friend since you've planted yourself so firmly in her space.

(5): Eye-Candy Iris

Yum! When you open the locker door and spy your pics, it's a definite mood lifter. You like being seen as somebody who's got great taste in guys—which anybody who passes your open door can see.

What this means: You've got a major romantic streak. Seeing those pictures lets your mind drift to, say, your dream of getting backstage passes to the Backstreet Boys' next concert. Just make sure to leave a little room on that door for the pic of a real-life sweetie—true love is way more fun than celeb crushes.

(6): Thinking-Ahead Tara

Know that Girl Scout saying "Be prepared"? Of course you do. You know that by keeping a jacket in your locker even when it's ninety degrees outside, you'll be set in case there's a freak drop in temperature.

What this means: You're game for surprises and last-minute plans, but you've got a good head on your shoulders, which means you don't take unnecessary risks. You probably almost always do your homework and get good grades.

(7): Last-Minute Lisa

Procrastination is the name of your game. You'll get to it tomorrow—and then you never do. It's not a conscious thing; you'd just rather have fun now and deal with the yucky stuff later.

What this means: You tend to put off tackling your problems until they've turned into giant messes. But with a little work you can overcome this, um, stinky habit.

(8): Get-to-Know-Me Gwyneth

You like to surround yourself with images that match your personality, whether it's radio station stickers or cute, cuddly kittens. It helps you get to know people who have similar interests, like when somebody who's cruisin' through the hall spies your No Doubt sticker and starts chattin'.

What this means: You may be a little shy, but you so want to make new friends that you came up with this ingenious plan. Good work! However, the fact that you stuck stickers in your locker (which are almost impossible to remove) means you could probably be a little more conscientious with other people's property.

4. What kind of smart are you?

Did you ever notice how you naturally excel in some subjects—and how you struggle in others, no matter how hard you try? It isn't because you aren't spending enough quality time with your textbooks. It's because everybody has mental strong points—and areas that need extra work. Take this quiz to find out your special strengths!

DIRECTIONS: Circle all the statements that sound like you.

 Sometimes I meditate or just sort of drift off in my own little world.

 I can figure out the 15 percent tip in a restaurant, no problem.

 I often get a song stuck in my head and can't get rid of it.

★ When my friend is in a bad mood, I can easily cheer her up.

◗ People say I tell great stories.

● I'd much rather do a project by myself than share the work with others.

▲ I'm not at all klutzy.

★ I can usually talk people into doing what I need them to do.

❖ People ask me for help with science experiments.

▲ I'm almost always in motion, tapping my foot or drumming my fingers.

★ It's really easy for me to look at a problem from the other person's point of view.

✦ I have an incredible sense of direction and rarely get lost.

◗ I never forget the punch line to a joke.

■ I know how to play an instrument, and I enjoy doing it.

● For me, answering the question "How do you feel?" is supersimple.

★ Within the first sixty seconds of talking to someone, I can tell what kind of mood they're in.

❖ I know at least ten of my friends' phone numbers by heart.

▲ I often act on my gut reaction instead of thinking it over.

◗ I'm really good at crossword puzzles and word games.

✦ I never forget a face, but sometimes I flake on the name.

★ People tell me that I'm a great listener.

✦ I'm good at picking out the right lipstick colors for my friends.

■ I prefer listening to the radio to watching TV.

● There aren't many topics that I don't have an opinion on.

❖ When there's a contest to guess the number of pennies in a big jar, I can usually come pretty close.

✦ When I take photos, people are always amazed at how well they turn out.

▲ I couldn't imagine not being able to play sports for a year.

◗ I love reading, and I understand books on the first read.

★ If the kid I'm baby-sitting doesn't want to go to bed, I can usually talk him into it.

✦ I can find the hidden image in those 3-D optical illusion posters.

■ I have a good sense of rhythm.

● I've always known what I want to do for a living when I grow up.

▲ I pay attention to what people say with their body language.

■ People say I have a nice singing voice.

❖ I can do math problems really quickly in my head.

■ When I hear at least three seconds of a song, I can almost always name that tune.

❖ I've taught myself to use new computer programs.

◗ My teachers have complimented me on my writing.

● When I get a magazine, I flip right to the quiz

because I love finding out more about myself.

 I'm really good with my hands, and detailed work comes easily to me.

◗ Speaking in front of crowds doesn't stress me out.

✦ When I give someone directions, I usually don't know street names, but I can give lots of landmarks.

Now add up the number of times you selected each shape and read the scoring section that corresponds with the one you selected most. (If you have a tie between two shapes, it means you display more than one kind of smarts, so go ahead and read the answer sections for both!)

Number of ●s: _____
Number of ■s: _____
Number of ▲s: _____
Number of ★s: _____
Number of ✦s: _____
Number of ❖s: _____
Number of ◗s: _____

IF YOU SELECTED MOSTLY ●s: **Self Smarts**

Looking inside yourself and figuring out your feelings comes easily to you. That's a great skill, because it means you know what it takes to make you happy—something many people have trouble figuring out. Also, you don't fall for your own excuses when it comes to procrastinating about schoolwork. You make a habit of challenging yourself to grow and reach new goals, which is a cool and rare trait.

Your answers indicate you would make a great . . . counselor, self-employed businessperson, psychologist, yoga instructor.

IF YOU SELECTED MOSTLY ■s: **Music Smarts**

This trait comes from so deep inside that you can't imagine life without it. You have a knack for knowing good music, and some people with this skill are capable of making great music, too. When you dance, you immediately find the beat . . . unlike the bazillions of poor, rhythm-challenged folks who have to concentrate (and still look like they're trying to stomp out a forest fire). If you have patience on top of this inborn music skill, you could have a great future in teaching this art.

Your answers indicate you would make a great . . . musician, singer, talent scout (a person who tries to find new talent for record companies), music critic.

IF YOU SELECTED MOSTLY ▲s: **Motion Smarts**

You are incredibly in tune with your body. When you're tense or stressed, you can feel it in your muscles—but you can still manage to make them perform the way you want them to. While many people freeze up when they're nervous, you're able to maintain the appearance of physical calm—even if your heart's beating like a lawn mower. You move with grace and rarely lose balance.

Your answers indicate you would make a great... surgeon, athlete, masseuse, coach, dancer, personal trainer, lifeguard, dance teacher, model.

IF YOU SELECTED MOSTLY ★s: **People Smarts**

Because you're a great listener (betcha scored high on that quiz!), you're really in tune with other people's emotions. So everyone knows that they can relate to you and trust you, which makes them feel great. You can use this skill in lots of ways—to teach, to give great speeches, to help win you a seat in student government.

Your answers indicate you would make a great... teacher, newscaster, politician, public-relations exec, radio deejay, psychiatrist.

IF YOU SELECTED MOSTLY ◆s: **Art Smarts**

You see things in a way that few people do, noticing colors and patterns that others miss. Also, you use this talent to make your own world a prettier place, whether it's by decorating your bedroom or doodling on your book covers. Art smarties like you usually dress with an artistic flair, putting together a cool look that's different from everybody else's. And your strong powers of observation don't go unnoticed by friends! They appreciate it when you comment on their new haircuts or cool shoes.

Your answers indicate you would make a great... photographer, architect, artist, interior designer, magazine art director, movie cameraperson, fashion designer.

IF YOU SELECTED MOSTLY ❖s: **Logic Smarts**

People with logic smarts can land seriously profitable jobs, since the computer industry needs people who understand patterns and complex math probs. You're great at figuring out problems that stump everyone else, which can lead you to invent some pretty amazing stuff.

Your answers indicate you would make a great . . . scientist, engineer, doctor, computer programmer, software designer, inventor, banker, stockbroker.

IF YOU SELECTED MOSTLY ◗s: **Language Smarts**

You're the one who tells great jokes in homeroom or entertains everybody with silly stories from your weekend. You can also put a serious spin on this talent, letting your word-crafting skills help you create great essays, stories, and poems. The words you use will always have a special artistic style.

Your answers indicate you would make a great . . . comedian, professional public speaker, salesperson, lawyer, author, journalist, screenwriter.

6

all about
your family
and home

ah, family—can't live with 'em, can't move 'em into the garage and claim the whole house for yourself. The vibes you pick up at home—loud or quiet, cramped or neat—are major factors in the person you become. With the quizzes in this chapter, you'll learn what your home base says about you and how to make it a perfect place to be!

1. What does your room reveal about you?

How you organize your private space says a lot about you. So are you calm and tidy—or one big mess? This quiz will reveal the truth.

1. There's hardly any open space on the walls of your bedroom.
True: Go to 2   *False:* Go to 3

2. When you take off your clothes at the end of the day, you usually put them away ASAP.
True: Go to 5   *False:* Go to 4

3. There's a color or theme that rules your room; most of the stuff in there matches.
True: Go to 6   *False:* Go to 5

4. The only time you really clean your room is when your parents use the words *grounded* and *pigsty*.
True: Go to 7   *False:* Go to 8

5. You have a real passion for decorating, and you see your room as an ongoing artistic project.
True: Go to 6   *False:* Go to 8

6. Your room looks very similar to the way it looked two years ago.
True: Go to 9   *False:* Go to 8

7. No matter how hard you try, you can't seem to keep your room clean.
True: Go to Cramped Cave   *False:* Go to 8

8. Friends are always saying how your room is totally "you."
True: Go to Stylish Space   *False:* Go to 10

9. There's rarely anything on your dresser except a few knickknacks.
   True: Go to Decorator's Dream *False: Go to 10*

10. Friends would be afraid to spend the night on your floor.
   True: Go to Cramped Cave   *False: Go to Decorator's Dream*

Decorator's Dream

Your personal space is like a museum—everything's perfectly positioned and very tidy. Taking care of your stuff comes pretty naturally to you. In fact, even your closet is probably organized by color and season. But in your quest to be neat, have you stripped your room of personality? Your room should look like you live there—not like it came straight from the IKEA catalog. Try these tips to personalize the place:

❊ *Put up a few framed pictures of friends.*

❊ *Leave out a piece of sports equipment—a soccer ball, ballet slippers, a field hockey stick.*

❊ *Make a mini-veg-out area with a beanbag chair and a stack of cool magazines.*

Stylish Space

Your bedroom is like a work in progress—always changing to reflect your moods and interests. People can get to know you a lot better by checking out your personal space. For example, when you've got it bad for a certain celeb, you make cute-boy wallpaper out of his posters. Or when you're stressing over school, people would find stacks of books (and okay, a few zillion Snickers wrappers). It's cool that you've claimed your space. When it gets outta-control cramped, remember these pointers:

✱ *Always try to make your bed—even if you just pull up the comforter. It fools parents into thinking the room is clean.*

✱ *Make a dedicated homework area—a desk or night table—so you don't lose important papers or forget to bring books to school.*

✱ *Put up a few cool hooks on the walls to keep you from throwing your robe or jacket on the floor.*

Cramped Cave

Yeah, we know your life is busy and that you have zero time to fold clothes. However, you're really making your stressed-out self even more stressed by allowing your room to be this disorganized. By walking two steps and, say, putting your shoes in the closet instead of leaving them in the middle of the floor, you save yourself time (and maybe even a stubbed toe). You'll probably also realize that you have lots of nice stuff that you'd forgotten about. To get a little more tidy, try these tips:

✱ *Ask your parents to buy you a hamper. A large one. Put all clothes in there the minute you take them off unless they're rewearable (admit it—we all do it).*

✱ *Eliminate these words from your vocab: "I'll do it later." Who are you kidding? You won't do it later. Take the extra two seconds to do it now.*

✱ *Make your room a no-food zone. Dirty plates and half-filled glasses can draw seriously icky bugs.*

Feng Shui–*ize Your Space*

Want harmony and balance to ooze from your bedroom? Follow these tips and learn the ancient Chinese art of *feng shui* (pronounced "fung shway") to make your space more blissful.

* Do keep the space under your bed clean. Having junk under there can make your sleep less restful.
* Don't put your bed near a window—your energy might escape during the night.
* Do take advantage of the natural knowledge zone in the northeast corner of your room. Put your desk there for good study energy.
* Don't let your desk get messy; it will make your thoughts cluttered, too.
* Do keep a plant in your room—its life force is contagious.
* Don't cheat and go for a fake plant or flowers; you can't soak up life force from dead things.
* Do ensure that you'll have great dreams by sleeping with your head at the north end of your bed.
* Don't sleep with your feet directly pointing at the door. It saps your energy.

Do You Know What Your Sleep Style Reveals?

The position you veg in for eight hours every night shows the world your deep, internal instincts. So try to match the most common sleep positions with the personality traits they reveal.

On your back
On your belly
Stretched out on your side
Curled up on your side
Constantly in motion

A. You're a pro at close relationships if you sleep this way. You're very sensitive, and you need lots of love and security.

B. Worry much? Thought so. Your sleep style reveals that you've got so much going on in your brain and a deep desire to reach your goals.

C. Everybody loves a mellow girl like you. You're the master of compromise, and you don't like to shove your opinions down people's throats. In fact, you're great at just going with the flow.

D. Where's the spotlight? Usually on you, you wacky extrovert. You're supersocial and don't mind being the center of attention. In fact, you'll often do anything for a laugh—even make yourself look silly.

E. People who snooze this way are majorly dedicated. Since it's a hard position to get into and out of, it indicates that you like things a certain way. You're private and organized, which means you let very few people get close to your heart.

Constantly in motion, B
Curled up on your side, A
Stretched out on your side, C
On your belly, E
On your back, D
Answers:

2. Youngest, oldest, middle . . . Are you true to your birth order?

Are you the first, middle, last, or only kid in your family? Researchers say that the order you were born in greatly affects your personality. But are you true to those birth-order traits? Read this and find out!

DIRECTIONS: Check all the statements that sound like you.

- ☐ It drives me crazy when my friends are late. ★
- ☐ I'm good at hiding it when I'm scared. ●
- ☐ I can usually talk my way out of trouble with teachers. ●
- ☐ I have a hard time saying no to people. ★
- ☐ After a tense situation, I often wish I'd spoken up. ✦
- ☐ People say that I'm a show-off. ●
- ☐ When I have a lot to do, I make a to-do list. ★
- ☐ I'm good at hiding my embarrassment. ✦
- ☐ Sometimes I stick with a boyfriend or crush even though I know he's treating me horribly. ✦
- ☐ I like being the center of attention. ●
- ☐ I won't go out if my outfit looks bad. ★
- ☐ I could do better in school if I tried. ●
- ☐ I sometimes think my family doesn't make me feel very special. ✦
- ☐ When it comes to compromising, I'm a pro. ✦
- ☐ I live by my date book. ★

I have a hard time sharing my thoughts and feelings with others. ★

People always say I'm "too young" for this and "too old" for that. ◆

I like playing team sports. ◆

I hate it when people don't take me seriously. ●

I often get lost in my own thoughts. ★

I'm very affectionate toward my friends and family. ●

SCORING

At the end of each statement is a shape. Count up the number of times you checked off a statement with each shape.

Number of ★s: _____
Number of ◆s: _____
Number of ●s: _____

IF YOU SELECTED MOSTLY ★s ... **You Show Qualities of an Oldest or Only Child**

The good side: You're ultraorganized, and just about everybody sees you as a leader. Also, you show so much maturity that people often think you're way older than you really are.

The bad side: You love being involved so much that you tend to get in over your head. When you feel like you might drown in work, just know that it's okay to say no.

IF YOU SELECTED MOSTLY ◆s . . . **You Show Qualities of a Middle Child**

The good side: You're amazingly understanding and so easy to get along with, and that makes you a great referee. When it comes to seeing an argument from both points of view, you're a master.

The bad side: Because you're so good at feeling other people's pain, sometimes you space out on having your own needs met. Remember, your happiness is just as important as everybody else's!

IF YOU SELECTED MOSTLY ●s . . . **You Show Qualities of a Youngest Child**

The good side: Hello, sunshine! Spotlight lovers like you are majorly fun to be around. You know you're cute, and you use that to your advantage, charming everyone within eyelash-batting distance.

The bad side: Ever notice how you skip out on responsibilities? When it comes to taking praise, you're front and center—but when it comes to taking blame, you're nowhere to be found. Just because people don't expect much from you doesn't give you an excuse to skate through life without doing hard work. Challenge yourself more often.

3. Do you know how to handle your parents?

Are you always fighting with the parental units? Does it seem like they were put on this earth to make you totally nuts? Well, there's a certain winning way of dealing with moms and dads—and it could make your life way easier. Answer these questions to find out if you're parent savvy.

1. Your best friend's curfew is a whole hour later than yours, which seems insanely unfair of your parents. Which strategy are you most likely to use to convince them to change it?

(a) Tell them everybody else is allowed to stay out later.

(b) Ask for an extra fifteen minutes, and come in on time.

(c) Wait for them to raise your curfew; they'll do it when they think you're ready.

2. There's a pair of boot-cut jeans you must have—but they cost $30 more than you have in your wallet. How do you improve your chances of getting money from your parents?

(a) Beg for the money and tell them to deduct it from your allowance.

(b) Ask if you can do extra chores to earn the cash.

(c) Hint that you'd reeeally like jeans for your birthday.

3. While in the middle of a great convo with your crush, call waiting beeps. You click over, and it's one of your mom's friends—and she says it's important. How do you handle her?

(a) "Can you call her back later?"

(b) "Can she call you back in five minutes?"

(c) "Can you hold on while I get off the other line?"

4. You're hosting a slumber party, and as your parents head off to bed, they say, "Absolutely nobody out of the house tonight." So when a group of boys shows up at the front door an hour later, what do you do?

(a) Tell everybody to be really quiet as you leave for a midnight walk.

(b) Say hey, then tell 'em they have to leave unless they want to see your pic in tomorrow's obituary section.

(c) Refuse to answer the door; they shouldn't be trying to get you in trouble like this!

5. Your room looks like a tornado ripped through it—followed by a really bad hurricane. So when Mom says, "No TV until it's clean," how do you deal?

(a) Seriously contemplate a TV-free life while you put off cleaning. It's your room; why can't you leave it the way you want it?

(b) Stuff junk in hiding spots—in the closet, under the bed—until the room looks presentable.

(c) Slip on your Walkman (and maybe some rubber gloves) and put your things away.

6. When it comes to your friends, your parents

(a) are kind of clueless or dislike most of them.

(b) like some of them and cringe at the sight of others.

(c) are totally supportive. They know (and approve of) most of your buds.

Count up the number of times you selected each letter, then read the answer section for the letter you selected most.

IF YOU SELECTED MOSTLY A'S **1 Percent Angel**

Your secret parent-controlling power: Ah, you've figured out how to raise begging to an art form. You'll continually ask (and ask . . . and ask . . .) for something until your parents give in (or go crazy).

The bummer for you is: You don't get the concept of "earning" something—respect, trust, that extra $30 for jeans.

Next time, try: When you find yourself on the verge of begging your parents for something, try stating your case calmly instead. For example, if you're asking to stay out an extra half hour, tell them why you need it and what you'll do in exchange. As in, "The movie doesn't let out until midnight, so I can be home by twelve-thirty. Next weekend I'll be in by eleven-thirty to make up for it."

IF YOU SELECTED MOSTLY B'S **50 Percent Angel**

Your secret parent-controlling power: You aren't afraid of a little work, and that earns you their legitimate respect. You know how to ask politely, and you've proved to the parental units that you can handle responsibility.

The bummer for you is: You feel bad pulling tricks on your parents because you know how disappointed they'd be if they found out.

Next time, try: Don't toy with your parents' trust. If you're considering breaking a rule, ask yourself if it's really worth the price you'll have to pay—grounding (easy) or rebuilding that trust with your parents (way hard).

IF YOU SELECTED MOSTLY C'S: **99 Percent Angel**
Your secret parent-controlling power: You're the ultimate rule follower, which makes you a parent's dream! You do what they say without asking questions or voicing your objections.
The bummer for you is: You often don't get what you want because you're afraid to question authority.
Next time, try: You need to learn to speak up for yourself, girl! Right now you sit by and wait for your parents to reward you for good behavior. But you need to look out for your own happiness, too! If there's a special circumstance, such as a camp-out slumber party or a dance that ends at one A.M., go ahead and ask your parents to consider letting you go. Most likely, with a little convincing, they'll trust you enough to bend the rules.

conclusion

all about your life

With each checkmark and circle you've made on the pages of this book, you've gotten to know yourself a little better. And we're not just talking about your guy-Q. You've beefed up your friendship skills, learned what your own special skills and talents are, and even figured out how to make life at home smooth sailing.

so now what?

Start working. These quizzes are just the beginning. By taking control of your life and turning yourself into the person you really want to be, you'll show the world serious confidence—and you'll feel more secure in your own skin, too. And no matter what your guy-Q, there isn't anything more attractive than knowing you're all that.